All Ratings Authorized

All Ratings Authorized

THE EXTRAORDINARY FLYING CAREER OF
CAPTAIN HARRY BERNARD

W. Baxter Byrd

W. Baxter Byrd

All Ratings Authorized
Copyright © 2005 by William Baxter Byrd. All rights reserved, including the right to reproduce this book or portions thereof in any form or by any means, electronic, mechanical, including photocopying, recording, or by any information storage and retrieval system, without permission in writing from the author.

Photos courtesy of Eddy Frankiewicz, Harry Bernard, Aviation Research Information Corporation, New York Daily News, Ralph Pettersen and Douglas E. Olsen.

10 9 8 7 6 5 4 3 2 1

This book is for those wonderful people I met along the way who made my journey much lighter. They are too numerous to mention individually but they made my trip so much easier.
Captain Harry Bernard, USNR Ret.

When once you have tasted flight, you will forever walk the earth with your eyes turned skyward, for there you have been, and there you will always long to return.
-Leonardo da Vinci

CONTENTS

	List of Illustrations	xi
	Preface	xiii
	Acknowledgements	xvii
	Author's Note	xix
1	New Haven	1
2	Africa	17
3	Navy	37
4	Reserves	75
5	Whirlybirds	99
6	CAA	125
7	Golden Years	145
8	Epilogue	153

LIST OF ILLUSTRATIONS

Harry on fountain in Miami
Pan American Airways training center, Miami
Harry at Graduation of Class 42A
Harry's crashed C-47, French Equatorial Africa
Second view, crashed C-47
Log Book entry, Africa
Harry and Norine on wedding day
Harry and his father, 1945
Naval recognition of Harry's B-17 sighting
(continued)
C-53 Harry flew when he spotted downed B-17
Harry's Civil Aeronautics Administration license
S-55 helicopter Harry flew while in New York
Harry as skipper of HS832
New York Daily News front page with crash headline
Harry at the office, Kennedy Airport
The DC-3 in which Harry was involved in his last crash
1975 National Transportation Safety Board on DC-3 crash
State Port Pilot article about drug aircraft
Harry and Twin Comanche
Harry and Baxter Byrd recording book
Baxter Byrd, Harry and Joan Bernard
Baxter Byrd and Harry

PREFACE

There will be fewer and fewer stories, the likes of which you are about to read, to come out of aviation again. You have already read about sound barriers that have been broken, altitudes whose bars have been raised and that Burt Rutan built an airplane that can touch the face of space and return safely to Earth.

This book deals with none of those issues. Books have already been published extolling the exploits of such events, and I won't add to the mound of trees needed to tell their stories again. Rather, this will be a story of one individual whose name you won't recognize but the events in which he was involved you most certainly will. There are no heroes in this story, although some of the events were heroic. There are no daredevils whose shenanigans in the cockpit were for purely thrill-seeking or record-breaking reasons, however some of the events involve stunts that would make Lloyd's of London think twice about insuring such an attempt.

Harry Bernard learned to fly in a world that had just barely given birth to aviation when one brother held his breath and hurled another down a rickety track in the sands of Kitty Hawk, North Carolina. Although it was quite abbreviated, it proved that indeed man could strap himself into wings of fabric and fly, if not quite like a bird, at least some semblance of one. Harry, in his youth, formed wings of fabric and although they were mere models of the airplanes that he had seen in magazines of the day, he knew one day they would be large and would take him high; his grandmother had told him so.

From his first solo at age nineteen, his new passion would take him proverbially around the world more times than he can recall. Among those trips were his share of trials and tribulations and close calls. He claims to have been saved by the skin of his teeth so many times that he is now on his second set of dentures. Although I cannot vouch for that, there are many tales of harrowing adventure, some of which nearly cost him his life. And there are undoubtedly more close calls that could have fit into this manuscript had the sixty-plus years of his flying not blurred the edges and allowed his subconscious to let them pass into quiet oblivion. Notes were not kept extensively at the time and only brief entries in his logbooks serve to spark memories long since extinguished by time.

Through a world war and a conflict, over the belly of Africa and the frigid North Atlantic, from the cockpit of more than 120 different types of airplanes and helicopters, logging over 35,000 hours of flight time, does his story take shape. He was there, and his stories are filled with firsts whether they were set out to be or not. They are not told from one who sat comfortably behind a desk all day and whose imagination has brought such events to light. They are true stories told in the true sense of history and have shaped a man and to some extent a burgeoning industry that was just getting off the ground. Sorry for that one…. Suffice it to say that Harry knows what he is talking about.

Although I have researched available sources to cross-reference facts, there is only a certain amount one can do trying to reconcile conversations that were held under duress and in the cockpit, with no voice recorders going and no NTSB to report to. As you get to know Harry, you will see that his intentions, even when speaking not so gloriously about someone, are that of telling the story, as it happened for good or bad. He never states that he is perfect or that he has never made a mistake or a bad judgment. There would be no advantage in doing so; it just isn't necessary. They are the facts as he knows them and far be it from me to begin to dispute them; so be it.

This book is the result of a rather lofty idea that struck me, I still to this day contend, in a fit of madness back in 1998, when I suddenly got the urge to write a book. All I needed was a subject and if I could harness some of the stories that I had heard bits and pieces of about my uncle Harry, I figured I just might have a chance. So it was the winter of 1998 that I moved to Oak Island, North Carolina, just a forty-five minute drive to North Myrtle Beach, South Carolina, where my uncle lived with my aunt Joan on the fairway at the Robber's Roost golf course. That wasn't by mistake, by the way. If there was a number two passion for Harry, it would be chasing a Titleist across the Bermuda.

I figured the beach would be a wonderful spot to start a book, but why I chose the winter to start I don't know. It was probably lucky, though, because during the summer the view of the beach may have been distracting with all the silks and the scent of coconut oil on the ocean breeze. I dunno....

Weekly, I traveled to see Harry and he would greet me at the door, along with his Labrador, Bogart. We would sit and sip hot tea with a splash of milk and generally act like old friends catching up the years and all the while I would be recording the conversation to be pecked out later at my beach home at a ratio of one hour recording to three hours transcribing.

We talked into the evening until about 6:00 P.M., when we would wrangle Bogart, I would gather the recorder, and we would head off in Harry's diesel Mercedes to the airport. When we arrived, Harry would drive across the ramp and park just along the edge of a large open field, whereby he would let Bogart run until white foam lathered his tongue. All the while, we would talk and on occasion Harry would spot a bird or two and name them with incredible accuracy.

Harry is somewhat of a legend at the airport, and, although he labels himself the president of the airport bums, his credentials are much more favorable than that. Pushed back in the corner of one of the hangars is Harry's airplane, the "other" woman; a 1964 Piper Twin Comanche that Harry has flown for close to thirty years. He designed the paint scheme, and the interior holds a vast array of avionics from GPSs to storm trackers to autopilot. Harry says it may be the best outfitted Twin Comanche in the world.

After more conversation with his bum friends and another long glance at the airplane we head off, back to the house to drop off Bogart and then meet my aunt Joan at the local K & W cafeteria for supper. Then back to the house where more tea was sipped and memories were magnetically remembered.

On occasion we would peruse the sun room whose walls were littered with plaques and commendations and awards. Also, there were autographed photos from names you would recognize, the Thunderbird precision flying team and one, which was mounted over his bed, the black and white picture inscribed, "To Norine and Harry Bernard, with best wishes from Igor Sikorsky." Harry knew Sikorsky when he was in the FAA ... but I'm getting ahead of myself.

In writing this book, I do not proclaim myself to be either a great aviator whose experience spans the globe, or Pulitzer winning author in the process of penning the Great American Novel. Rather, I am one who happens to know someone I think you would want to know too, who is lucky enough to call Harry uncle and who was lucky enough for him and his wife to let me intrude in their lives for three months a few years ago. I hope you think so too.

ACKNOWLEDGEMENTS

The author wishes to recognize and thank all of those who have made this book possible:

My wife Chandra, thank you for your love, patience and understanding while I spent my many hours in my cave working.

My parents, Charles and Sandy who encouraged me from the beginning and whose support has always been a rock from which I have stood all these years.

My brother Bobby for letting me squat at the beach house with him in the winter of 1998-99 while I conducted interviews and pecked out the words that came from them.

Commander Eddy Frankiewicz who so graciously contributed story after story of his and Harry's friendship, and whose pictures have brought life to many of the names and events in this book.

My aunt Joan for letting me be a welcome guest in her house all those Wednesdays, and gave constant encouragement and information during the entire project.

To Harry, whose hours of stories kept me on the edge of my seat at times and brought tears to my eyes at others. And who helped me understand what it was like in the good ol' days, I shall never forget.

AUTHOR'S NOTE

All Ratings Authorized is not an arbitrary title to this book. When Harry entered the Civil Aeronautics Administration as an air carrier inspector in 1947, he was required to fly many different types of aircraft at a moment's notice, many of which were in the process of being certified themselves. Instead of requiring a type rating for each and every airplane flown, the CAA covered this by stating on the license, "All Ratings Authorized," giving the inspectors permission to fly nearly any aircraft carte blanche. At the time of this writing, Harry estimates there are fewer than a hand's worth of pilots with this license still flying.

1
NEW HAVEN

There is no better place to start with Harry's story than right at the beginning. As you will see, it didn't take long for Harry to be exposed to the activities that would dominate his life. I mentioned earlier of how his grandmother once foretold of Harry's fate when he was a child and when I asked Harry to tell me of his childhood, that is the story he told me first. Whether or not the declaration was a premonition or simply an offhand remark, it was true enough that Harry ended up exactly as his grandmother said. I clicked on the miniature tape recorder and as the tape began to feed, he started....

"I was born in Lochee, Dundee, Scotland, January 22, 1920. People are often asked what their first memory is and sometimes that is a hard question to answer. It's hard to determine whether that incident is actually your earliest recollection or it was an incident that happened to you when you were young and it was told to you many times and that is what you are remembering. I was three years old and of course we lived in Scotland, and we lived on the second floor of what was called a close, now called a scheme. I climbed up on the railing of the balcony and was balancing myself, walking across the railing, when my mother grabbed me and kept me from falling to the ground. At that time my grandmother and my great-grandmother lived with us. My grandmother was a fairly large woman with white hair and always wore black. In those days almost everyone wore black. Well, she made the comment, 'That boy will go high in life.' I guess that was an omen or intuition. And that's what I did with my life; go very high.

"During the years following World War I, the economy was real bad in Scotland like it was in most of Europe. As a result, my father, who worked in the insurance business, and I guess my mother as his partner decided to take the family to America, 'Where the streets were paved with gold.' Following the custom in those days, he came over by himself first to get a job, and worked for a year to earn enough money to send for the rest of the family.

"We set sail on the SS *Cameronia* and I think we sailed steerage, which is the lowest possible cost for passage. We landed in New York Harbor on December 23, 1924. I was four years old, my brother Andrew was a year older and my other brother David was a year younger. My mother brought us over together with my grandmother, 'Granny,' we called her. She had always lived with us. She was a widow, her husband died in 1908 when he went to India to build a jute mill. He built a plant and installed the machinery and was teaching the local people how to run the factory when he died and was buried in Calcutta.

"When we came to this country I apparently had the measles. Well, you can't enter a country with a contagious disease, so I was suppose to go into quarantine but my grandmother smiled at the health inspector and said, 'Oh, he's only flush because he just woke up from his nap,' and she talked him out of it. So I always like to tell people I got in this country illegally.

"When it came time to get us through, the immigration official called out the name 'Bernard' with the accent on the second syllable and nobody answered. He called out the name 'Bernard' again and again nobody answered. So he spelled the name B-e-r-n-a-r-d. My mother said, 'That's us the Bernerds.' So we got in and eventually got tired of telling people how to pronounce our name; it was a lot easier to answer to Bernard than to explain to people it is Bern*e*rd.

"We settled in New Haven, Connecticut, where my grandmother had a sister who had come over several years earlier and was living, and we stayed at her home until we found a place of our own. My father had been hired as a gardener; I believe it was for the president of Winchester Repeating Arms. During that time, we rented a little house on Clark street in New Haven. It was owned by an Italian family by the name of D'Onafrio, who were very, very good to us; the three boys, my mother and father and my grandmother.

"One day Mrs. D'Onafrio came over with a pot and she put it on the stove and said to my mother, 'Do you like cabbage?' Well, asking the Scotch people if they like cabbage is like asking a ten-year-old boy if he likes ice cream. Cabbage was one of the staples of the Scotch diet along with brussel sprouts, mutton and boiled potatoes. Mrs. D'Onafrio visited for a while and had a cup of tea, no one came in our house without a cup of tea. After she left, my mother went into the kitchen and we heard her scream. 'Granny, Granny come here quick!' We all followed Granny into the kitchen and all had to smell this cabbage that had turned bad. My mother swore us to secrecy, 'Don't tell Mrs. D'Onafrio, we don't want to insult her.' And she wrapped it up in some newspapers and tied it up with twine. When my father came home from work that evening, he took the three boys and marched half a mile down the railroad cut and he dumped this cabbage that had turned bad down the railroad cut. It turned out to be sauerkraut, but we had never heard of sauerkraut, that was something new to us so we thought the cabbage had turned bad."

"My father had a great sense of humor. I often tell some of his stories and I'll tell you one right now.

"This young fellow was hauled into court in Dundee for arson. And the judge wasn't sure what arson was. He called up the defendant before the court and said *(Harry breaks into a thick brogue)* 'I've given the mattah a lot o' thought, and I've decided that you're going to have to marry this girl! There is too much of this arson going on!'"

We both laughed and Harry raised himself from his easy chair and went into the kitchen to fix a cup of tea. While he walked he shook his head a little and continued to chuckle at his father's joke.

Harry also spoke of his grandmother's great wit as well. One story surrounded the abdication of the throne by King Edward VIII on December 10, 1936. He had been once divorced and according to the rules of the Church of England, if he were to marry again, he could no longer carry the crown.

Well, the king was about to give his speech on the radio and in those days the signal strength isn't what it is today and there was a bit of a wait until the signal cleared up and the king would again try his broadcast. In the meantime, during the wait, Harry's grandmother went up to her room to knit and told Harry's mother to call her when the king was on. The signal cleared and the announcer came on to introduce the king and Harry's mother yelled upstairs, "Granny, Granny, come down quick, the king is here, the king is here!" whereupon Granny's soft voice fell down the stairs, "Oh, that's fine dear, won't you invite him in for a cup of tea?"

It was easy to see where Harry got his quick wit and sense of humor after listening to a few of the family's stories.
He also told me of his first date with my aunt Joan at a local Myrtle Beach Chinese restaurant. They sat, in a dimly lit booth, sipping hot green tea and making small talk about this and that. The conversation soon turned to Harry and he spoke at length of his distinguished flying career, his interests and hobbies. This went on until after the main course had been served and looking up from his plate of Kung Pao chicken, Harry said, "Well, I've talked enough about myself... what do YOU think about me?" Joan laughed and knew she would find great joy with this fellow, even though he was a bit stuck on himself.

Harry returned to his story and told me of how he became interested in golf, another of his lifetime pursuits.

"At one time we lived on the site of the first golf course built in New Haven. It had been abandoned, it was no longer a golf course, but it was still wide open. There were only two houses on it and we were one of the two. As a result we used to do a lot of hitting golf balls back and forth and I guess by the time I was ten or eleven I was caddying at the country club, we had since cut holes in the ground and played on the old course. It wasn't in very good shape but it was where we learned to hit the ball properly. I found a golf club in the tall grass when I was about ten, in those days the rough wasn't anything like it is today. It wasn't a question of whether you were going to have a golf swing or be against a tree, the rough in those days was knee high and you were lucky to find your ball.

"In the tall rough one day I found a golf club, in fact it's up there in that rack."

Harry pointed to a rack that held a dozen or so wooden-shafted clubs, some with their leather-wrapped grips unfurling.

"It was quite an old club when I found it; it had to be thirty or forty years old and that was in about 1930. It was called Elephant brand, a phosphor-bronze putter.

"Monday was caddy day at the golf course; members couldn't play on Monday. We would show up at daybreak with some old clubs and a bag of sandwiches and play until it got dark, and that's how we learned the game. We always had a caddy house and the caddies who were not carrying bags would putt for pennies on hard-pan dirt with a hole cut in it with a #2 tomato can or something in there.

"In those days you got seventy-five cents for carrying a bag and you got a ten-cent tip if you were a class 'A' caddy. The caddies were class A-B-C-D. You brought home eighty-five cents, which for the depression was much appreciated at home. Nobody had any money, people worked for twenty-five cents an hour, which is ten dollars weekly and they were glad to get the work.

"Out on that golf course, there was a stream that ran through it and we dammed it up using old flour sacks filled with sand and we made ourselves a hockey rink for wintertime. Of course in Connecticut you skated and skied all winter long. Our first pair of skis we made ourselves with barrel staves. We would get an old belt and nail the belt to both sides and that would hold your foot in. Of course later we went to ski boots and binders but even then, they were pretty primitive. We played hockey in the backyard, we also had a baseball diamond we built in the summer with the neighborhood kids, so we learned how to field, throw and hit the ball. We played 'piggy-stick' where you hit a stick on the ground it would jump up and you would hit it like a baseball and run the bases.

"Then my father decided he was going to put in a bowling green behind the house. The Scots are very big with the bowls. The bowling greens are like putting greens in this country. He hired a black man who had a mule and a wagon and a plow to come plow the land to plant the grass for the bowling green. My brother Andy and I, while the fellow was plowing the land, were on the wagon seat heading west, snapping our whips at the horses to get them moving; playing westerns you know. Well, on the seat there was something that looked like a candy bar, but a little bit thicker. So we decided we were going to steal this candy bar so we each took a bite out of it. It was very, very hard and we started to chew on it. It didn't taste like chocolate but we ended up swallowing it because we didn't know what else to do. It was chewing tobacco. And I never put another piece of chewing tobacco in my mouth since that day!"

I asked Harry when he first became interested in airplanes and when was the first time he took a ride in an airplane. "That is an interesting story," *he told me, and began to enlighten me on his first forays into aviation.*

"My brother and I were very interested in airplanes. I really can't tell you how that started; there was no airport around there at all. But we were able to get aeronautic magazines that were very cheap in those days and they had plans for airplanes and my brother and I would build model airplanes out of balsa wood and tissue. We were reading everything we could about aviation, of course that wasn't long after Lindbergh astonished the world with his flight from New York to Paris, thirty-three hours and some minutes in May of 1927. I didn't know any pilots, or mechanics. I didn't know anybody that had anything to do with aviation, but yet I had this interest in aviation and read as much as I could about it."

"One day when I was almost twelve years old, about sixth grade, I was sitting there in class and out the window I saw my first airplane, it was descending. I ran out of that classroom and chased that airplane through the woods, over the hills and sure enough it was landing. I got up to it shortly after he got down. It turned out to be an Englishman, named Williams, who was going to start a little barnstorming operation there, hopping passengers for $2.50. He was in an old Standard with an OX5 engine.

"I was coming up on twelve years old and my mother asked me what I wanted for my birthday and I said I wanted $2.50. My father was probably making twelve or fourteen dollars a week which was a pretty good wage in those days so $2.50 was a lot of money. She wanted to know what I wanted it for but I wouldn't tell her. So I didn't get the $2.50 from her, but my grandmother told me to come up to her room, and she asked me what I wanted the money for. Well, I could always tell my grandmother anything; I was her pet you see. So I said I want to take a ride in an airplane. 'You do son, eh. $2.50 is a lot of money.' But she gave me the money and I put it in my little fist and ran to the airplane and took my ride for $2.50, and I've been chasing airplanes ever since you might say!"

"In high school, I didn't perform so much in the athletic way because we went to Trinity Episcopal Church on the Green in New Haven and they had a parish house with a gym so that's where I hung out. I did a lot of gymnastics there and learned to play badminton and became very good at badminton. I was the New England State badminton champion one year. In gym class, my specialty was the parallel bars, I did a clown act on the bars, which everyone seemed to enjoy."

"It's interesting how we got to Trinity Church. Several blocks from where we first moved to in New Haven, there was a Presbyterian church, of course we were Presbyterian, most everyone in Scotland was born Presbyterian and the church was called the 'Kirche.' They took us up there the first Sunday, my mother and father and the three boys. Somebody got to talking with them and said, 'Well, put the three boys in those chairs and you can go into the service, and we will take care of the boys, and put them in Sunday school.' They came out an hour and a half later and we were still sitting there, nobody had paid any attention to us, we sat there like three angels waiting for someone to tell us what to do. Well, my father got so upset about that he said, 'If this is the way the Presbyterian Church treats the little boys, then they are not going to see me here again!'

"So we went to Trinity Church on the Green in New Haven. That was over two miles from where we lived, but my father had a car in those days and we managed to get there and that's why I grew up in the Episcopal Church.

"That is where I first got real interested in music; both my brothers and I were taking piano lessons. One of the first things my mother bought when we got to this country was a piano. She loved music, she was a wonderful contralto singer; had a beautiful voice. At all the Scotch times [parties] she would always have to sing a solo or a duet with somebody. She bought us boys lessons; they were twenty-five cents and the teacher was Ms. Grace Willughby Brown. Now, here I am seventy years later and I still remember that name. My grandmother used to always feel sorry for her for some reason, and she would always give her a cup of tea when she was finished with the lessons. We would play six-handed piano, not three people on three pianos but three people on one piano.

"Trinity Church had a wonderful music program, they had one of the world's major organs at that time. The church was built in 1752; they had an English choirmaster and organist named Harry Reed. I think he took a liking to me and gave me some lessons on the organ. I became a member of the choir, because I could read music and had a soprano voice. There were forty voices in all, the boys sang soprano and the men sang tenor and bass. I was paid $40 a quarter as a soprano and when I was about ten, I became a soprano soloist. Our choir was quite famous, we made records and traveled and gave concerts.

"When I was around twelve, one of the world's most famous organists, who was the organist at the Notre Dame cathedral in Paris, came to this country on a concert tour. He was going to play five concerts in America and one of them was at Trinity Church because of the major organ. Harry Reed, the choirmaster, asked me to turn the pages for Marcel Dupre. That was one of my greatest musical thrills, of which I will never forget; to sit on that organ bench and turn his pages."

What a treat for a boy of twelve! Marcel Dupre was indeed one of the greatest organists of all time. At age eleven he was appointed organist of the church of Saint-Vivien in Rouen, France, which was his birthplace. His incredible talent was demonstrated when just after World War I he gave a recital of Bach's complete organ works by memory.

Throughout his whole life he devoted himself entirely to the organ through teaching, performing and composing until his death in 1971.

"Incidentally, when I became a soloist my pay became $40 a month, $10 each Sunday. That money of course went to the family coffers. When Harry Reed died I was still the soloist and the new choirmaster was an outstanding musician named G. F. Huntington Byles. I was soloist for him for five or six months until my voice changed.

"I was very serious about my piano playing and when it came time to go to college, it was during the depression, and my father couldn't help financially but he said I could live at the house so I could get a job and bring in some money. In the meantime, I was studying piano and my ambition at the time was to teach American history either at the high school level or at the college level. I went to New Haven State College, which is now Southern Connecticut University, and is now probably 12,000 students.

"One year I went down to New York, to show the world what a great pianist sounded like. I took a room in the Sherman Square Hotel, on Broadway and 73rd street. It's no longer there but it was an old run-down hotel where all the run-down musicians came out to live. Some of them were of course has beens, some of them were wannabe's and some would never be. I took a room for $3.50 a week there and it was next to two Welshmen, Thomas L. Thomas and his brother D. Elwyn Thomas, we called him Dave Thomas. They had two cots, the sheets were gray and bags of garbage and stacks of music sat along the walls and were covered with dust, but right in the middle of the room was a Steinway grand piano with not a bit of dust on it. I had a lot of fun doing music with them. I did get a job in 1939, as a rehearsal pianist for Morton Downey, he was the star of Billy Rose's Aquacade, which starred Billy Rose's wife Eleanor Holm who was a champion Olympic swimmer in those days. However, I found out that there were thousands of pianists in New York all of whom were a hell of a lot better than I was so I decided to aim my career in some other direction."

Harry has always maintained his interest in music, playing for churches and singing groups throughout his life. Before we move on to other subjects, I will introduce you to a story that has become near legend in the North Myrtle Beach, South Carolina area. Harry had been playing organ for a group called the Testimonials at the Lakeside Baptist Church in North Myrtle Beach. They were asked to play at a fellowship meeting and when they finished their singing, Harry gathered his music and prepared to leave the bench when the pastor, Jim Mezick, stopped him and asked him to play a little something while they bowed their heads in prayer. The rest, I'll let Harry tell....

"Well, if you have ever seen your best friend and can't remember his name, that's what happened to me. My mind went completely blank. I don't play by ear so I have to have music in front of me, that or I have to have memorized it, one of the two. So I just didn't know what to do in that situation, but I looked up and everybody had their head bowed waiting for me to do something and I said to myself, 'Bernard, you have got to do something!' Well, I couldn't think of what to play, not even 'Stand up, Stand up for Jesus,' or 'Onward Christian Soldiers.' So in desperation I sat down and played 'Smoke Gets in Your Eyes.' But I played it very reverently. It was the only song that popped into my mind; it was a song I had memorized years before. So I played it and put a nice little 'amen' at the end of it thinking some of the people would overlook the song I was playing if it had a nice 'amen' at the end of it. Well, when I finished, Jim Mezick said, 'That's beautiful, a little unusual, but beautiful and maybe that's a reminder not to let the devil put smoke in our eyes.'"

Now back to the early years and some fond memories of a job that enabled Harry to stay in school and eventually begin flying.

"The following summer, between my freshman and sophomore years, I had one of the best jobs I have ever had at the Raceburg Country Club. It was one of the oldest clubs in southern Connecticut and it had a beautiful clubhouse; it was huge. They had an apartment on the second floor for the club manager, his wife and daughter and they spent the summers at the beach, so the club hired me to babysit the clubhouse during the summer. A typical daily routine would be to get up early, gather all the trash in the club station wagon and take it to the dump, come back and get the shopping list from the chef for the food he needed to run the dining room that day and night. Then I would go down to the market and buy the food; the lobsters, the whole filet mignon strip he told me how to find a good one and evaluate it. I would deliver it all and that would probably take two hours. So that meant from 10:00 A.M. on I was free for the rest of the day. Now when you are interested in golf, if you had the day off and could play for nothing, naturally I would spend the day playing golf. I was free until 9:00 P.M. and in the meantime I could have my meals in the kitchen prepared by the chef, then I relieved Ernie the bartender and I would serve drinks to the members while they played cards or slot machines. I had to stay there until the last member wanted to go home and often that would be the wee hours of the morning and he would be too drunk to drive so I would have to drive him home. I would then close up the bar and do it again the next day. I did that seven days a week and made enough money to go back and start my senior year of college."

"I went back to history and that is what I was studying when I learned how to fly in a program called the Civilian Pilot Training Program or CPTP, which was a program started by Roosevelt who saw the war coming on in Europe and decided that we were going to train pilots. They had two pilot programs, one on the east coast and one on the west coast. They gave the one on the west coast to Stanford University and Yale was supposed to take over the one on the east coast, but Yale didn't want the program so they gave it to our little college. The program was so successful that they started CPTP programs all over the country and they trained probably tens of thousands of pilots. If you talked to an airline pilot ten years after the war chances are fifty percent that he would be ex-military and fifty percent that he was trained in the CPTP."

During this time, Harry would strike up a friendship that to this day is still as close as ever. Eddy Frankiewicz and Harry were in the second phase of the four-phase CPTP program, and because of the usual camaraderie that occurs around aviation, they became quite good friends and study mates. Harry, being from the New Haven area, lived with his parents, but Eddy was from Rutland, Vermont, and at the time was living in a small brick boarding house close to the airport. Until this time, Eddy had been receiving financial support from his father, but as a letter from his sister detailed, Eddy's father was becoming less and less interested in Eddy's plans to become a pilot and so the money would no longer be available for Eddy to pursue his studies.

Being in a bind, Harry and Eddy began to wash and detail cars as a job to make enough money to pay for the books, tuition, ground school and food. However, it became obvious that there just wouldn't be any way for Eddy to be able to afford to continue at the CPTP program. He would have to quit school, and quit flying.

In the middle of all this, Harry spoke with his mother about Eddy's financial problems and asked if there was any way he could stay with them and thus be able to keep flying. Harry's mom agreed. His two brothers had gone to the Army and there would of course be room for one more at the house. Eddy recalls, "I remember turning away from Harry so he wouldn't see the tears in my eyes."

Eddy and Harry would fly. More importantly, they would fly together.

The two, along with several of their classmates, now all friends, completed all four phases of the CPTP program and were designated flight instructors as well as receiving their commercial flight certificates. This would prove most advantageous in their quest for excitement in the skies.

"They had given that program to a psychology professor, I think he was head of the psyche department, his name was Jess Neff and he knew I was interested in airplanes and in fact I had a little flight time. I had taken some lessons in a Piper J-3 Cub for $3.50 an hour, but I wasn't much of an expert in aviation.

"When I got in the CPTP program we had the primary phase, the secondary phase, the cross-country phase and then instrument phase. If you went through all four phases you wound up with a commercial license and an instrument rating. The fixed-base operators eventually took them over and they used J-3 Cubs or Taylorcraft for the primary. The secondary was acrobatics and a lot of them used Waco UPF-7s or Myer OTWs or Great Lake trainers. Then for the cross-country a lot of them used the Stinson 108 series and finally on instruments you were in a Stinson Reliant.

NEW HAVEN

"My first cross-country was an interesting flight and was from Bridgeport, Connecticut, to Augusta, Maine, on a day that was very hazy, it wasn't raining, it was just hazy. Well, somehow I found Augusta, landed and had someone sign my logbook saying I was there and on the way home the visibility deteriorated and I became lost. But how lost can you get if you keep the Atlantic Ocean on your left! I couldn't see the Atlantic Ocean and that's why I got lost. In those days all of the towers were on the frequency 278 kHz, so you always kept your radio tuned to 278 kHz. I knew I was somewhere in New England when I heard the Boston tower, Logan, tell an American Airlines flight to be careful because there is a little red bumble bee that seems to be lost up there and not to run into him. So I knew that I was over the Boston airport and I was able to find my way home.

"At that time it was hard to find the Boston airport because they didn't have runways. It was just a huge plot of land covered with black cinders. What would delineate the runways would be these cement squares 100 feet square where you ran up your engines so you wouldn't pick up cinders in your engine. Then you turned your airplane and aimed it at the square maybe 4,000 feet away and that was your runway. When you land you pick out a concrete square, line up with the opposite square and use it as a runway. At that time I don't believe there were any paved runways in Massachusetts. I know there were no paved runways in Connecticut. Hartford, Brainerd Field, was the air carrier airport at the time and it was grass surrounded by a high dike to protect it from the high waters from the Connecticut River. We would come up from Bridgeport, up the Connecticut River and practice our night landings and takeoffs at Brainerd Field. But if the airport attendant heard an airplane he would turn on floodlights, they didn't have runway lights, and you would be charged $1.50 for use of those floodlights. So we would come up the river at low altitude and sneak in below the top of the levees around the airport and come up and land before he had a chance to put the lights on."

"Between my junior and senior year in college I got a job with the Bridgeport flying service, which was owned by a dentist by the name of Joe Levy. I got a job teaching acrobatics in the CPTP secondary in a Waco UPF-7. Friday was payday and all the instructors got paid on Friday except me. So one morning I went to see Joe and I said, 'Hey doc I didn't get my paycheck,' and he said, 'Harry don't worry about it.'

"Well, the same thing went on the following Friday and the following Friday. I never earned a damn dime but he knew I wouldn't quit because I was trying to get 300 hours to get a job with Pan Am Airways. Years later after World War II, when I worked for the Civil Aeronautics Administration [CAA], I had a meeting up in Bridgeport with Joe and some other people about expanding the airport. After the meeting we went to lunch and I sat next to Joe and I said, 'You know Joe, I worked all summer long for you in 1940 and I never got paid for the whole summer!'

"He looked at me and said, 'Harry, don't worry about it!'"

With their new ratings and 300 hours of flight time under their belts, the boys were eager to make their mark in aviation. Soon after their graduation, they heard about Pan American Airways' desire to hire new pilots and received invitations to the Chrysler building in New York City.

2
AFRICA

In June of 1941, Pan Am began negotiations to support the British army and the U.S. Army Air Corps with a trans-African air route. The route ran from Bathurst, Gambia, on the west coast of Africa, literally straight across the thickest part of Africa to Khartoum, Anglo Egyptian Sudan. From there the routes split, one going north through Iraq then down the Persian gulf to Karachi, India, now Pakistan, the other continuing south from Khartoum, skirting the southern coast of Yemen and Oman on to Karachi. From Karachi, some flights proceeded to fly "The Hump," the Himalayan Mountains, and on into Chungking, China, which is another whole story in itself.

What is now known as Pan Am-Africa provided a much-needed resource in men and machines to support the war effort against the Axis powers. They hauled men and arms, ammunition and sometimes dignitaries on their way to meet with presidents and diplomats. Although the Pan Am-Africa contract was relatively short lived, it existed for eighteen months until its military takeover, there is no doubt that without the effort and quick response of these men, the war in North Africa could most certainly have taken a turn for the worse.

AFRICA

Back in Connecticut, Harry had just finished his first semester of his senior year in college, which would be December 1941. Harry continues....

"At that time I was working as a part-time flight instructor for the Bridgeport Flying Service in Bridgeport, Connecticut. The word went around that Pan Am was hiring pilots if they had 300 hours of flight time and a commercial pilot certificate. I had the commercial pilot ticket and more than 300 hours so Eddy Frankiewicz and I took a train down to New York and went to the Chrysler building where Pan Am had its headquarters. The chief pilot was a fellow named 'Brick' Maxwell. 'Brick' because of his red hair. He interviewed us and ten minutes after we walked into his office, we had signed a contract to be junior pilots at $100 per month to report to Miami for training right after the holidays."

Harry's good friend and Pan Am classmate, Commander Eddy Frankiewicz, tells the story of their fun-filled trip to Miami.

"It was almost too good to be true; we were to receive Pan Am training in Miami! Six of us from Connecticut were being sent from the winter of New England to the sunshine of very southern Florida. I was from Rutland, Vermont, and had never been farther away than Pennsylvania.

"A great adventure unfolded as four of us, Harry Bernard, Don Swanson, myself and Len Eagles, owner of a circa 1937 Plymouth sedan (no trunk), with all our luggage departed Connecticut for Miami just after New Years, 1942. What a joy! What camaraderie! Harry and Don had attended a movie the night before featuring Dinah Shore singing 'My mama done tole me, etc.,' and they regaled Len and me with repeated renditions of this and other songs Dinah sang.

"We spent the first night in Petersburg, Virginia, at a very fine hotel I believe named the Hotel Petersburg. It had a very attractive Old South lobby and dining room and our waiter was black in a black suit wearing white gloves. None of us had ever eaten in as fine a dining room as this. We all ordered T-bone steaks, rare, except me who had never ordered a steak in my life and I ordered it well done like my mother always cooked it. Needless to say I was unanimously shamed into ordering it rare and I sure did like it cooked that way, even to this day fifty-seven years later!

"The second day was even more enjoyable, seeing new countryside, farms, villages and the piney woods. A sad scene dampened our spirits however at a crossroad in the deserted countryside. We came upon a terrible automobile accident with bodies strewn about, fortunately covered with blankets. We spent that night in Savannah, Georgia, enjoying the evening. The final day of driving was spent along the Atlantic coast of Florida. Len let us share in the fun of driving and even loaned us his Ray Ban Aviator sunglasses as we drove.

"We arrived in Miami late that night and rented rooms in a boarding house on Biscayne Boulevard, and fell asleep immediately. The next morning we drove to the Terrace Club, NW 119th Street, in the Opa Locka area of Miami that had been taken over by Pan Am as our living and classroom quarters. The Terrace Club was plush! Spacious grounds, semicircle driveway, circular stairways to the second floor with huge crystal chandeliers in the high ceilinged dining room. The rest of our class, Class 42A, numbering thirty-two guys arrived at about the same time and we quickly established a close rapport and fellowship."

What followed were four months of intensive training including ground school, radio and celestial navigation and Morse code, in which thirteen words a minute, transmitting and receiving, were needed to satisfactorily complete the course. It's odd, but that is about the same speed at which this author types....

They flew the North American AT-6 advanced trainer. Being powered by a Pratt and Whitney 550hp Wasp engine, it was easily the most powerful plane any of them had flown and must have been quite a thrill compared to the Waco UPF-7s and the Stinson SR-6s they were used to. Harry even got to fly a blimp; Poopy Bags they called them. Instrument flight training was performed in the single-seat

AFRICA

"Link" trainers. But school wasn't all books and formulas and studying as a story from Eddy illustrates.

"Of course on our time off, we would explore the various beaches and night spots of Miami and the surrounding area. At one beer joint, Zizzon's Bowery, red-checkered tablecloths full of discarded peanut shells were shaken brusquely in the faces of newly arriving customers. Strategically placed air hoses would blast air up the skirts of unsuspecting female patrons giving the males in the room a most enjoyable treat. Also the ladies room had a surprise. A life-sized painting of a nude male was painted on the wall in front of the john. A one-foot square flap was placed over the private area of the painting with a sign that read: 'Do not lift this flap.' Now what red-blooded gal could resist such temptation? When she lifted the flap, a loud horn sounded and a red flashing light came on above the flap opening on the customers' side of the wall and there she was, most startled looking out at the customers."

I have never gotten out of Eddy how he knew exactly what was in the ladies room of that particular bar....

"On April 24, 1942, the first class of thirty-two pilots was graduated as Class 42A. And guess who graced the head table representing Class 42A with Pan Am president Juan Trippe at his left? None other than our favorite, Harry Bernard. This pattern of Harry acting as master of ceremonies has been repeated without exception at Pan Am and Navy squadron reunions and adds longevity to a persons existence by creating joyous belly laughs!"

During their time in Miami, they had a recreational officer of some note, Robert Crawford, whom some of you will remember as the creator of the Army Air Corps song. "Off we go into the wild blue yonder...." Harry remembers that Bob wrote another song that wasn't quite as popular, in fact not many people have heard it at all. Harry graced me with a short verse, "Oh, we're the mech's of the

Air Corps, nuts to you, mud in your eye, we're the guys that make 'em fly!"

Whether that was to be an official song or not I cannot say, although Harry did remember the mechanics used to hum it frequently.

With four months of rigorous training under their belts, Class 42A was now ready for departure to Accra, British Gold Coast, now Ghana. In May of 1942, just weeks after graduating, Harry, Eddy and a handful of their classmates boarded a China Clipper Boeing 314 bound for Africa. What thoughts stirred their imaginations one can only guess, but I am sure a bit of trepidation had to be included. After all, they were only half the world from home and had all of their possessions tucked neatly into a duffel bag.

Not long after they arrived in Africa, James Doolittle performed his daring raid on Tokyo, weakening Japanese defenses and generally instilling fear in the Japanese and confidence in the Americans. Many of the pilots who were involved in the raid flew back to America over the trans-African route. Although Harry never actually carried Doolittle himself, he did carry several of his crew members. One such name he remembers is Richard Knobloch, who was the copilot of lucky plane number thirteen, which dropped bombs on docks and ships in Tokyo harbor.

Harry now picks up the story beginning with what was going to be their hometown for the foreseeable future, Accra.

"Accra was a wonderful experience for me; I loved every minute of it. They had built new barracks out of cement blocks, and they had three pilots to each room. We each had a single mahogany bed, and two drawers of a six-drawer dresser. We also had a houseboy, which we paid three dollars a week for keeping our clothes clean and pressing them, his name was John Worke. He was a wonderful fellow, but under British Colonial rule, although he held a degree as a graduate, he could not hold a meaningful job. It was similar to the blacks in this country at one time. We had a mess hall and the food was not gourmet type food by any means. I survived on bread and peanut butter and the barrels of flour had worms in them. When we first got over there we would take a fork and dig out all the worms but after a week or two we would just ask for the 'raisin' bread and smear it with peanut butter, we figured it was just extra protein for us. We called the natives 'wogs' and after you finished your meal the wog would come up and say 'Sweet, master?' for dessert. I eventually got used to the food; it wasn't all that bad. On the layover stops we would have Nile River shad and sometimes gazelle, which wasn't too bad.

"The route went from Accra, west to Bathurst in Gambia, back east to Freetown in Sierra Leone, then back to Accra. Then from Accra going east, one of the first obstacles we would run into would be Lome, which was Vichy French territory and it was a supply base for German submarines. Next was Lagos, the capital of Nigeria, and from Lagos we went up to Kano, the largest walled city in the world. Although we had no navigational aids, if the weather was good we didn't need any because Kano was the center of radiating trails in all directions. Camel trails, walking trails, all kinds of trails and all you had to do was to follow these trails right to the city. The route then went to Maiduguri in the northeast corner of Nigeria, and east to Fort Lamy [now N'Djamena]. Fort Lamy was what we called a flag stop. Meaning we only stopped there if we had someone to drop off or pick up. It was free French area and the French had a requirement for anyone that had a trading license, they would lose the license if they ever ran out of prophylactics or whisky. So they had great warehouses of Canadian Club whisky, which we would buy for a dollar a bottle. Somehow we always managed a flight into Fort Lamy, which at that time was the capital of French Equatorial Africa, now the country of Chad. From there we went to El Geneina, then El Fasher, then into Khartoum, which was the capital of the Anglo Egyptian Sudan, now just Sudan. Then the route split and we headed north from there up the Nile River to Luxor, Egypt, and into Cairo."

I would like to interject that the preceding description of the routes Pan Am flew was recited by memory and is more than sixty years old.

"I had one trip and one of my passengers was an editor of a very popular magazine back home who shall remain nameless. We had an overnight stop in Luxor, the home of many Egyptian antiquities such as the Temple of Carnac, The Colossi of Memnon, King Tut's tomb and the Valley of the Kings. The Luxor Hotel, which is where we stayed, had a bar called The American Bar. The bartender was a wonderful character by the name of Ali Assiz, and he had a big sign over the bar, which read, 'Drink Ali Assiz's gin fizz, the best gin fizz which is!' Well, I'll tell you, he could make gin fizzes, but it was so hot you had to drink two or three just to quench your thirst and then the fourth one knocked you off your stool! We are sitting there, enjoying our gin fizzes and the aforementioned nameless editor of that American magazine says to me, 'Do you think we could get some women tonight?'

"I said, 'Oh yeah, prostitution is legal in this country, it is handed down from mother to daughter!'

"Well, in the light of the full moon in the village square they would have all of the girls come out and do their dances of the seven veils and one thing or another. All the men and women would sit around watching these performances and if you particularly liked one girl you would go up and pinch her on the ass to tell her what a wonderful dancer she was. There was an old fat guy there, a merchant, he was too fat to get up so he had a little boy that was sitting cross-legged on the ground and he would nod to which girl he liked and the little boy would run up and pinch the girl on the ass for him."

I guess they had no child labor laws at the time....

"Anyway, we went outside and hired a gharri, which is a horse-drawn taxi and he took us down to what we would call in this country the red light district. It was quite late, probably around midnight, and the driver parked the gharri underneath a street lamp and he yelled, 'Ish matalahane igigibaya moya americano!' Well, all the lights came on and the girls came out and surrounded the carriage. The driver then pointed out how much each girl costs. In those days, the Egyptians used the pound and there were a hundred piasters to one pound. One piaster equaled four cents, making the pound worth about four dollars. He would point out, twenty piasters, ten piasters, and five piasters. So I took the twenty-piaster girl; I figured she would be safest.

"Off we go up to her home and there was an old windup Victrola playing some old Egyptian record."

Harry now proceeds to imitate the sound of this record, which sounds something like that alley cat that always seems to be just out of shotgun reach and a door hinge that is in dire need of an entire can of 3-in-1 oil.

"The whole time this girl is sashaying around the room and the mother and father and I were sitting at the kitchen table dickering over the price. First, they brought out a bottle of wine and there I am, having wine on top of all those gin fizzes. Then we start to discuss the price, and we must have discussed that price forever. After probably an hour of discussing back and forth, they finally agreed to the twenty piasters, eighty American cents, which is what the gharri driver said she was worth. Well, I didn't have any change and the smallest thing I had was an Egyptian pound. They wanted to keep the whole pound and I said, 'No, no, twenty piasters, give me change.' They didn't have change, so they woke up the little brother, and he left with the pound and he went around to the different girls until he had enough change for the pound, he came back and they gave me eighty piasters change, keeping twenty piasters, then they left."

Jeez Harry, 80 cents! Big spender! Hell, compared to what a night out fetches these days, that's a bargain at twice the price! But I guess what was waiting for Harry in the morning shows the gharri driver was just about right on the price.

"I got into bed with her, which was sort of like a bunk with wooden sides and well…. When I woke in the morning and oh boy there is nothing like a headache in the morning, this girl was still sleeping. She woke up and what had been a fairy princess the night before was knocked several notches down! In fact, it scared the hell out of me when I looked at her face because she had one eye that had gone white from gonorrhea! Oh man, she looked so beautiful the night before I couldn't understand how she could get so ugly overnight! I went around to locate my nameless friend and he was out to the world, but I got him because he was going up to Cairo. Luckily he hadn't had the same misfortune as I."

"In Cairo, we stayed in the old Shepheard's Hotel, which later burned down and a new Shepheard's Hotel has taken its place. It was the center of activity for all of the Europeans. It had a huge, wide veranda and rocking chairs and the most wonderful service. We would sit there and watch Cairo go by and on the street they would have a raree, which was a street circus with animals, and sometimes fornicating animals, monkeys and things. We would chat and talk, then go shopping. They had wonderful prices on Chanel No. 5, which I always bought when I was there. We would also do the tourist things, go see the Sphinx and Pyramids and we would go to the Mena House sometimes."

The Mena House might ring a bell with history buffs as being the place where Roosevelt, Churchill and Chiang Kai Shek met to discuss the invasion of Europe. Originally built by the king of Egypt as a royal hunting lodge, the hotel has been home to some of the most famous, or infamous politicians, actors and celebrities the world has known. Its reputation still survives as a premier hotel to this day with its backdrop of the great pyramids providing a romantic and awe-inspiring view to its visitors.

"We also had staff house in Heliopolis, which is a suburb of Cairo. It had a balcony and we would sit there at night, drink beer and watch the German airplanes come over and bomb the airport every night. Their army would then work all night filling in the holes and the airport would never miss a beat. There was a train that ran from Heliopolis down the middle of the street into downtown Cairo. It had six or eight cars and there were a couple of guys that got drunk one night and stole a huge English military truck and they pushed that train all the way into downtown Cairo. They never let it stop, they just pushed it all the way into Cairo!

"From Cairo, we headed across the Suez Canal into Jerusalem and there was a special procedure to cross the Ismaila corridor. They used what they called the 'Color of the day system,' which was a code of a certain sort where for certain hours of the day, say four hours, you would shoot off red and green flares to let the defenders know that you were friendly aircraft. They actually shot down an Army Air Corps DC-3 because they didn't shoot off the 'Colors of the day.'

"Some of the guys had a good thing going there. There was a pretty red-haired girl that everybody knew that was married to an English soldier up in Jerusalem. She would always be a passenger on our flights from Cairo to Jerusalem; she would spend a day or so and then fly back on the next flight. Well, those pilots became very, very good friends with her and she always returned the favor! There is nothing like a red-headed Jew, by the way...."

"On one flight from Cairo we were going to Jerusalem and then up to Damascus, back to Jerusalem then we would RON [remain over night] for fifteen days at a hotel. Not having any navigational aids, we got caught in what is called a Harmatten wind. That is a dust storm where the dust can go as high as 12,000 feet. Visibility is zero except for straight down, there was no slant visibility at all. We had trouble finding the airport and had a load of English army people. We had a brigadier general, some lesser rank and some enlisted people, so there were sixteen or eighteen in total. We went back to the brigadier and told him that we would have to return to Cairo because we couldn't find the airport. He said, 'Well, I have a map of the Holy Land, maybe we can find it on this map.' He was reading a National Geographic that had a map of the Holy Land where Jesus walked, so we used that map to find the airport.

"We would then fly into Damascus, Syria, or south into Baghdad, Iraq. There were two other stops in Iraq as well, Basra and Habbaniya. Things were very hot in that damned Iraqi desert. On a return trip one time, we landed in Basra, and it was so hot, I believe it was 135 degrees in the sun. Of course you had to wear gloves; you couldn't touch the airplanes because the metal was so hot. The DC-3 hydraulic system was a 1500-psi system and it had a thermal expansion valve in it. Well, it got so hot and the pressure built up so rapidly that the thermal expansion valve couldn't handle it so the copilot had to continuously work the landing gear lever up and down to relieve pressure to keep it from blowing up. When we would land, the airplanes would be taxied right from the hot sun into a hangar and we would leave the airplane there for the night to cool off. Interestingly enough, in spite of the heat, under irrigation, they grew the most delicious melons, the sweetest and juiciest melons I have ever tasted came from that area.

"From Iraq, we went to Qatar, the capital of Bahrain Island and to Tehran, Iran. We would spend the night there and then head back to Accra. Some trips went from Iran on to Karachi, India, then New Delhi, and Calcutta, and on into China, over 'The Hump' [Himalayas] into Kunming, China.

"Other flights from Khartoum flew up the coast of Arabia to Salalah into an island off the southeastern coast of Arabia called Masirah. We called it Misery Island. Nothing grew on the island; it was completely shale and rocks and sand, and a runway.

"We made a stop in there one time, and incidentally we always carried what were called 'blood chits;' these were American people that we got rewards for if we could find them. Arabia at that time, like the rest of the Middle East, was mostly warring Bedouin tribes fighting with each other. Well, they had guards stationed at that airport to protect us from the marauding tribes and I got to talking with one of the guards, well not exactly talking, I knew a little Arabic and we could make ourselves understood. He was carrying a knife, a shabaria, a curved knife in a beautifully hand tooled case and an old Lee-Enfield rifle with two crossed bandoleers of ammunition. I asked if I could see his knife and he hesitated like he didn't understand me and I said, 'knife, knife' and pointed to it. He finally took it out and handed it to me handle first, and I admired it. It was hand made, probably a foot in length. I said 'nice, nice' and handed it back to him handle first. He took that knife and drew it across his arm and drew blood with that knife, because the Bedouins are not allowed to draw the knife unless they draw blood."

One of the stops on the southern route from Khartoum was Asmara in the country of Eritrea. At the time, Eritrea was taken over as an Italian colony, which lasted until the end of the war. Eventually, Eritrea was returned to Ethiopia as a province. However, friction between Eritrea and Ethiopia eventually lead to Eritrea's independence in 1993 and was granted membership in the United Nations. Since then, Eritrea has had land disputes with its neighbor across the Red Sea, Yemen, but in 1996, both agreed to have the dispute settled by an international panel.

"In the Italian Eritrea, Mussolini built a wonderful resort for his officers, the Italians were very big with brothels and houses of ill repute. At this resort, you had to be an officer to get in, but we wore khaki uniforms with silver bars on our shoulders so they thought we were Army Air Corps officers. The equipment we were flying were all C-47s and C-53s which was the military designation for DC-3, all painted khaki.

"I went there one night and it was beautiful; you walked through a gate, identified yourself, walked through a sunken garden with colored lights flashing on the fountains, walked up the marble stairs into the big manor house. You go sit at the bar and pick out a girl, probably have dinner with her and you go upstairs, where you had to go through a clinic where the doctor examined you before and after.

"I was in the shower and at that time, it was my habit to sing Pagliacci in the shower."

Harry demonstrates with a short rendition of Pagliacci, his voice resonating throughout the house.

"I had a very good tenor voice at that time and unbeknownst to me one of my good buddies, Peter Goutierre, was also upstairs and as I was singing in the shower, he said to his girl, 'Ah, Pagliacci; Caruso!' and his girl said, 'Pagliacci, cie, Caruso, No!'"

Harry's eyes closed, his head reared back and filled the room with laughter.

"I met Peter walking down the hall to the clinic and he told me the story. I hired Peter later as an air carrier inspector at Washington National Airport and he spent a lot of his time over in Jordan and became very close friends with King Hussein, who just died [February, 1999]. In fact, the book he wrote, which was called *Himalayan Rogue* has a letter from King Hussein in the foreword for his book."

As previously mentioned, the pilots of Pan Am-Africa had very minimal navigational aids and most of them relied on one thing: clear weather. Whether it was celestial navigation, or simply VFR (visual flying rules), clear skies were necessary nearly all of the time. When the rains came, flying became a whole different story and getting lost was just part of the game as Harry explains.

"We had no navigational aids and very primitive communications, if any, using pilotage and dead reckoning to navigate. We had charts but they were all French and old from the last century and most of the land was colored yellow; the color used for unsurveyed territory. We mainly used geographical features: rivers, towns and oceans.

"On one of these trips I had a very interesting experience. I had a young captain, Will York, whom I think was as young as I was, maybe a year older; I was only twenty-two. We crossed the Indian Ocean in a monsoon, very heavy rains and high winds and we navigated up the coast of Arabia by using the phosphorescent. Most of the south coast of Arabia was a sheer cliff and as the waves broke against it, the white phosphorescent shone and we just followed that line. As we got closer to Karachi, this was a cargo flight, the weather improved and we were able to pick up the coast of India and the captain started to head north. I said, 'No, we are way north of Karachi; we need to turn south to get to Karachi. With that wind we had, we had to be blown north off course.'

"We got into an argument and he had his way because he was the captain. So we flew and flew, following the coastline and the next thing I know we are on a northwesterly heading, and then a westerly heading and getting low on fuel. He still insisted we were south of the airport, even though we picked up this westerly heading. You know, that is how people are when they are wrong, they are so sure they are right. He was one of these guys I would classify as, 'He wasn't always right, but he was never in doubt.'

"We were flying and I spotted an airplane on the ground, a Royal Air Force [RAF] Spitfire and we could see the outline of a runway marked on the gravel with 55-gallon drums painted yellow. We landed and it was a RAF base with one Spitfire and one officer, he was about as young as us, and I think there were ten enlisted men. We were not in the country we were aiming for; we were in the province of Baluchistan, northwest of our intended spot.

"They put us up for the night and the young flight officer said, 'To celebrate the Yanks; I have a special treat for dessert.' Everyone was gathered in the mess tent and he brought out a gallon full of fruit salad that his mother sent to him for a special event and he said that this was a special occasion.

"The next morning they loaded our plane with enough fuel to get to Karachi; they had a big stash of five-gallon tins of fuel all stacked up in huge piles. We headed back and got to Karachi in the middle of the morning and we didn't tell anybody we were yesterday's flight a day late, we just made believe we were that day's flight. The communications were so primitive in those days it didn't make any difference."

All in all, the trips that Harry made during his time in Africa went off without too much difficulty. However there was one time in particular when Harry wasn't sure if he would make it out of the Dark Continent at all. The next story is one of the first stories I can remember hearing from Harry and in fact, the first time I heard it I was twenty-two years old; the same age Harry was when this event happened.

"Hold on! We're gonna hit hard!"

Both copilots turned the yoke with tremendous quickness just as the right wing tip hit a most inconveniently placed tree. Spinning on a vertical axis, the C-53 loaded with .50-caliber incendiary ammunition hit the ground and came to a halt, resting within yards of the Ubangi-Shari River in French Equatorial Africa, now known as the country of Chad.

It is 1:00 A.M., July 13, 1942. Pan Am-Africa pilot Harry Bernard, his captain, and fellow copilot have just crash landed in what is quite literally, the middle of nowhere. Their mission was simple enough; carry a full load of .50-caliber ammunition to Cairo to support the British 8th army in defeating Rommel in the North African campaign. Simple considering this was to be one of the first night flights across Africa and simple considering the only navigational aids they had were the stars and dead reckoning; there were no GPS units along for this flight.

Harry's plane was one of three C-53s that night, loaded with ammunition planning to fly straight through to Cairo only landing for fuel. That was the plan at least. Harry picks up the details on what was to be a rather rude invitation to a long flying career.

"We took off, flying formation loaded with .50-caliber incendiary ammunition. The normal maximum gross weight of a C-53 was 25,000 pounds and we grossed out at 33,000 pounds! We landed at Accra for fuel; we couldn't take full fuel with all that ammunition aboard. Then Maiduguri, again only for fuel. The next stop was Fort Lamy, which was a huge French garrison and was where General Leclerc marched through the edge of the Sahara desert up to meet the British in the North African campaign. It was dusk when we took off and we were heading for our next stop, which was El Geneina. One of the big navigational points was a huge granite obelisk called the 'Camel's Dick,' at least that was our name for it. I don't know what the real name for it is."

In fact, the "Camel's Dick" is actually called Jebel Bara Simbal. Whether or not it bears any resemblance to an actual camel's dick I cannot say having never been privy to that particular view before. It was, however, a very good landmark in clear weather, being about as obvious to the pilots as the noses on their faces.

"Well, it was too dark to see the Camel's dick and we were trying to fly formation when we ran into thunderstorm activity. Pan Am had a procedure called airplot. That is where you hit your time and turn ninety-degrees to the right for so many minutes, then turn ninety-degrees left for so many minutes, turn ninety- degrees left again for so many minutes, then finally a right ninety-degree turn theoretically puts you back on your original track. Well, the only thing airplot did for us was to get us in the middle of a humongous thunderstorm. It was during this time that the formation was separated. Our captain had a nervous breakdown and was praying to God that if he ever got out of this he would never get into an airplane so long as he lived, so the two copilots ended up flying the airplane.

"We were flying along through this thunderstorm and we lost one engine, and we couldn't stay up there with that terrible gross we had on board. We lowered down; we were going to crash land someplace and I didn't know where we were. We spotted a river, which we could see because the river was slightly darker than the surrounding ground and there was also a small fire on the edge of it.

"I said, 'Well, let's go over the fire and do a 360 and come in and land in the river using the fire as our spot.' When we flew over, they doused the fire so we lost our spot and subsequently had to put it down the best we could.

"After we landed, we took stock of our situation, the airplane did not explode, we expected it to explode, and with all that ammunition you had better make yourself scarce! We were standing contemplating our fate when we heard voices coming through the darkness and there was a column of men with lighted torches and they surrounded the airplane, it was like a Frank Buck movie! They doused their torches and everything got quiet, very quiet. We had a flashlight, a Zippo lighter and a crash axe in the airplane so I went back to get them. I figured if they were going to do something, there was nothing we could do about it so let's show them at least that we were white men to show who we were. So I shined the light on us overhead and, 'Uumph,' they took off. But they slowly came back and I shined the light on us and again they ran off but they didn't go as far. After several times they finally just stayed there. So I thought, now it's their turn so I shined the light on them and they took off again, so I had to go through the whole procedure again.

"We had flown through a lot of countries and knew bits of a lot of languages. We tried English of course, I knew some Arabic, and then I tried French. I had two years of high school French and if you look at my records, I probably flunked that! So I began speaking French like a damn French native, and it turned out the chief of the village spoke French and I found out later that he was the only one who had ever seen a white man. He was kidnapped when he was twelve years old by the French and he was assigned to the salt caravans that moved across the south edge of the Sahara desert. The area we happened to be in was called the Sahel, it is a transition between the rain forest and desert.

"I told the chief, 'Revient demain,' (come back tomorrow). So we barricaded ourselves in the airplane trying to sleep in the stifling heat on wooden boxes of .50-caliber ammo. The hydraulic system, which was a 1500-pound system, was ruptured and every once in a while, 'Wheeee,' two pints of hydraulic fluid would squirt out and we would jump up and say, 'What the hell was that?' We also had an overhead antenna that ran over the top from nose to tail over the fuselage, and it would hum in the wind so needless to say, we didn't get much sleep that night.

"At the cold light of dawn, it being one in the morning when we crashed, we looked out and there they still were right exactly where we left them, just sitting on the ground circling the airplane. It turned out there were about 200 people in the village and about seventy or eighty were men. They wore a white cloth kind of like an abu, like the Arabs wore; knee length and a sash and they all carried spears and some carried swords."

These people belonged to the Sara group. They are primarily farmers both tilling the soil and raising cattle like their further eastern neighbors, the Masai. The Sara predominately inhabit the surrounding areas of the Shari and Logone rivers.

"I started a conversation with the chief and asked where Fort Lamy was and he would point in a direction and say (in French) a twenty-one day walk. So we figured out how far a man could walk in one day and then figured the distances for El Geneina and El Fasher. We then triangulated ourselves on a very minimal map we had.

"We tried the radios and they were still working. We called Fort Lamy first and couldn't raise them, so we called El Geneina and we raised them. They said they had several planes out all night looking for us, including some RAF aircraft, bombers and a couple of our DC-3s. One of the British bombers informed me he went up as high as he could and flashed his landing lights on and off in the hopes we could see him but we never did."

I can only guess that in fact the British and the other planes that were looking for the downed C-53 were not exactly hopeful in finding survivors at all. The chances of a C-53 loaded with incendiary ammunition crashing just east of nowhere and not exploding on impact to say the least was very lucky.

"It was about this time we saw a DC-3 headed westbound about twenty miles north of our position. Of course by this time the weather had improved; the thunderstorms had passed.

"I got the numbers of the airplanes that were looking for us and I assigned them each a cardinal heading. That particular plane kept flying west so I knew which airplane that was. I told him head due south about twenty miles, we were on the banks of a river.

"That airplane happened to be flown by a senior pilot for Pan Am-Africa, a fellow by the name of Hank Kristofferson. He was the father of the singer and actor Kris Kristofferson. He spotted us and dropped us a great canvas bag of canned food, all of which split open when it hit the ground. But that didn't make any difference to those natives they were scooping up that fruit salad and SPAM; they had never tasted anything like that before. They had tried to feed us with a gourd filled with milk from a cow and a couple of raw eggs floating in it along with dirt and leaves and twigs too. I drank it but didn't drink it all; I didn't want to offend them.

"Hank said there was a clearing nearby, and it looked like he could get the DC-3 in there if we could cut down some of the trees, he would be back. We got all the natives to help us, they had crude agricultural implements like hoes and picks and we had our axe. We worked everybody cutting down termite hills and in Africa the termite hills are sometimes twelve to fifteen feet high and are as hard as concrete. We broke them up as best we could, the trees were not heavy, mostly very small sapling type trees. We cleared a 1200-foot runway and they came back and Hank landed and rolled down about half-way when his left wheel went into a hole we had missed and the tail of the airplane went up and it looked like it was going to go over, but it didn't. It tottered there for a little bit and fell back down on its tail wheel. It was a good thing, because that was the airplane that was going to get us out of there.

"They flew us out and flew mechanics, sheet metal workers, hydraulic people, engine and propeller people and set up a base camp there that they called 'Bush City' and in about four weeks they flew that airplane out of there.

"When it came time to pay the natives for their work, they wouldn't accept vouchers and they wouldn't accept paper money. But they did take all of the coins that the group had. We were flying through so many countries and we always had coins in our pockets from the countries. So we put all of those coins together in a pile and that is what they wanted as payment.

AFRICA

It turned out to be about $12 worth in American money, so I guess you could say we built a 1200-foot runway in the middle of Africa for $12!"

Harry got a good laugh out of telling me that story. A broad smile came across his face as he looked back in time and recounted the events like they were yesterday, never mind the fact they were sixty-plus years ago!

Harry continued to fly in Africa until November of 1942 when the Pan Am-Africa contracts were almost completed and operations were gradually being taken over by the Army Air Corps. They offered all of the pilots to stay and fly their same routes, but it had been a long time since Harry had been home. Harry told them he would stay, only if he could have a few weeks home first for a little R and R. Well, the powers at large said "No" and so did Harry.

He hopped a flight back to Miami on a TWA Stratocruiser; "it wasn't a very good performer," Harry recalls, and landed on November 28, 1942. That happened to be the same night of the horrific fire at the Cocoanut Grove in Boston where 492 people lost their lives. The fire, believed to have been started by a lighted match used to change a light bulb, caused mass mayhem and when patrons tried to rush to the exits, they found only revolving doors. With people pushing on both sides of the revolving doors, they didn't budge. This resulted in the people in the inside of the building being trapped and overcome by smoke and fire as aghast onlookers outside of the building watched helplessly. This unfortunate circumstance gave birth to a new fire code for buildings with revolving doors that a standard, outward swinging door must be located adjacent to a revolving door and remain unlocked to prevent such a disaster from ever occurring again.

3
NAVY

After Harry arrived back in the United States in November of 1942, he was still officially working for Pan Am. He was assigned, for a short while, to a Boeing 314 Clipper as 5th officer, but, as Harry continues, that didn't last long.

"We flew from Miami to New York on a flying boat, the big Boeing 314; the Clipper Ships. That of course was the airplane that made Pan American. They were big four-engine flying boats and they had big sponsons off the bottom of the fuselage, stub wings they called them. So they assigned me as 5th officer on the Boeing 314 Clipper. They carried thirteen crew members: The Clipper Skipper, and five pilot officers, two navigators, two radio ops and the rest were stewards, we didn't use stewardesses, and the crew often outnumbered the passengers.

"The fellow that started Pan Am, Juan Trippe, was a Naval aviator and he fashioned his airline after a lot of the Navy procedure and protocol. When you landed, you caught your buoy and the boat came out to pick you up, the crew disembarked first and then the passengers. And then when everyone boarded, the crew boarded first. There was one bell for the crew and two bells for the passengers.

"In those days, a trip from New York to Buenos Aires took five days because Pan Am only flew in the daytime and only when the weather was good; they did not fly on instruments. The first day was from New York to Miami, which was usually eight hours. The second day we would fly from Miami to Trinidad, which is now Trinidad and Tobago, we would remain over night there, then the third day was Trinidad to Belen, Brazil, at the mouth of the Amazon River. The fourth day was Rio de Janeiro and the fifth day was Buenos Aires.

"Only two pilots were allowed to take off and land the Clipper. One was the Clipper Skipper and the other was the 1st officer. On the crew I was assigned, the 1st officer had received his fifteen-year pin from Pan Am. I said to myself, 'Holy shit, he's been working for fifteen years and he is still a copilot, how long does it take to get to captain?' My duty as 5th officer was to: First, keep the captain's room made up, second to sit on the flight deck in one hour tours watching the auto pilot, third to help the steward serve the meals, and act as a fourth if anyone wanted to play bridge!

"I couldn't see at the time how I could do that and enjoy it, so Eddy Frankiewicz, my buddy from the CPTP and Africa went to New York, after New Years, to the Naval procurement headquarters, which was 120 Broadway, in New York City. We filled out a few papers, and the procurement officer said to me, 'OK, we'll make you a Navy pilot, will an ensign be alright?'

"I said, 'An ensign, is that a commissioned officer?'

"'Oh, yes.' He says.

"I said, 'Oh, that will be fine.'"

If there was ever a time to be modest, this was not it.

"Well, Eddy was right behind me and the procurement officer said, 'Will an ensign be alright with you?'

"Eddy says, 'No, what's your next highest rank?'

"'A lieutenant, jg' [junior grade].'

"So Eddy said, 'That's what I want, a lieutenant (jg)!'

"And I said, 'Wait a minute I want a lieutenant (jg) too!'

"The officer said, 'No, you're already an ensign, sorry, go get some uniforms and you'll hear from us.'

"That was January 8 when we were sworn in the Navy, I was commissioned an ensign and Eddy was commissioned lieutenant (jg).

"One of our buddies, who was in the copilot programs, his mother was vice president of Lord and Taylor; a great big store in New York. We went to see her and said, 'We are here for uniforms.'

"She said, 'Oh, wonderful, come on I'll take you down to the tailor.'

"So we went down and he measured us and he said, 'How many stripes should I put on the sleeve?'

"I said, 'Would you put four stripes on my sleeve please?'

"And he said, 'You're a captain already?'

"I said, 'No, I'm an ensign.'

"He said, 'You only get one stripe if you are an ensign!'

"So I got one stripe and Eddy got one and a half because he was a junior grade lieutenant."

Harry and Eddy didn't have too much time to show off their fancy stripe to everyone. As Harry continues, he describes the events that ultimately ended with his designation as an "official" Naval aviator. Eddy remembers that they were in a unique position as they had not been indoctrinated into the Navy, but they knew how to fly and received flight pay, but didn't have their official Naval aviator wings. Quite a pair, these two, but it was just par for the course based on their rush order to Africa a few years earlier, they were ready for adventure and here they would find the next chapter.

Shortly after the start of the war in December of 1941, Secretary of the Navy, Frank Knox, established the Naval Air Transport Service with the first squadron being squadron VR1. Knox, quite a colorful character himself, served as secretary from 1940 until he died in office and was replaced by James Forrestal in 1944. He was a veteran of the Spanish-American war, having been a member of the "Rough Riders" as well as serving in WW I.

"I don't think we were home forty-eight hours when we got orders to report to active duty to squadron VR1, Naval Air Transport Service, in Norfolk, Virginia. The reason we went in the Navy was to be fighter pilots down in the Pacific so we could kill some of those damn Japanese! Somebody had injected us with a hypodermic needle full of the Star Spangled Banner, I mean we were gung ho! I said, 'VR1, that's a transport service, we're going to be flying transports?'

"We met the skipper for squadron VR1 and he said, 'What the hell are you guys doing here?'

"I said, 'We got orders to report here.'

"He said, 'Well hell, we can't use you, you're not a Naval aviator!'

"I said, 'What do you mean I'm not a Naval aviator? I'm an aviator and I'm in the Navy, doesn't that make me a Naval aviator?'

"No, no you've got to go through flight training and be designated as a Naval aviator, we'll get this straightened out.'

"I was talking to the operations officer, a commander named Fitzgerald, he said, 'He is so short on pilots, he'll use anybody, he will use you guys.'

"So we got signed up for operations, no paperwork or anything, that's where we worked. It was ninety days before it got squared away, and in the meantime I flew, in those ninety days, something like thirty different types of Navy airplanes, fighters, seaplanes, even a J-3 Cub. The Navy called them NE-1s it had a pod on the side of it for carrying the wounded out of the battle areas."

Harry's partner Eddy Frankiewicz interjects with a short demonstration of their greenness.

"We were standing in the lobby of the air operations building, when a single engine aircraft came to a screeching halt outside. The canopy was abruptly shoved open, a Navy captain jumped out, came dashing in and said to me, the first person he saw, 'Where's the head?' I answered, 'Up those stairs, second door on the right.' Just about immediately he reappeared and snarled that, 'The second hatch on the starboard up the ladder was the commanding officer's office and where the hell is the toilet, you blasted Feather Merchant!' I hurriedly pointed and said, 'Right there,' but I didn't dare ask him what a Feather Merchant was."

During this time, Harry flew, what he called, "all kinds of missions." From ferrying airplanes, to flying the mail, or flying up to eighteen- or twenty-thousand feet taking temperature readings. One set of orders he won't readily forget called for Harry to fly an admiral to Rhode Island during a spot of bad weather.

"Right next to the air station was the Naval Amphibious Training Command headquarters in Little Creek, Virginia. One day I got orders to carry the admiral to Quonset Point, Rhode Island, in a Grumman Goose. That morning I went down to check the weather and it was stinking all the way up and down the east coast. In those days they classified the weather sequences as, 'C' for contact, which is VFR, 'I' for instruments and 'X' for closed. Well hell, everything was 'X,' so I came back to Commander Fitzgerald and said, 'We are going to have to scrub this mission, everything is closed because the weather is stinking.'

"He said, 'Yeah, I agree with you, call the admiral's office and tell them we will cancel.'

"I called the admiral's office and his aide said, 'You can tell him yourself, he's on the way over there!' So I went back down to the ready room and was playing acey-ducey, and the squawk box comes in, 'Ensign Bernard, report to Commander Fitzgerald immediately!' I got down to his office and he introduces me to the admiral. Well, I'm not in the Navy very long and I said to myself, 'Gee whiz this is nice, I get to meet all the admirals and everything.' We chatted small talk for about three or four minutes about various subjects and actually called one another by our first names, which you never do. Finally the admiral says, 'Ok, ensign let's go.'

"I said, 'Lets go? Let's go where?'

"He said, 'Quonset Point, Rhode Island.'

"'We are not flying that today,' I said, 'We scrubbed that mission because the weather is so bad.'

"'You have got to get me up there, I've got to be up there in the morning for meetings!'

"Then Commander Fitzgerald starts backing him up and says, 'You heard the admiral, get going!'

"So I figured if he's willing, I'm willing.

"The admiral had an aide with him, and we got in the airplane and took off and I figured shit, it's no problem I'll just let down over Cape Charles and just follow the Atlantic Ocean all the way up. Well, I never saw the ground after I left; it was solid instruments. When I thought I was near Cape Charles, I let down a little bit, almost in the tree tops and was trying to find something I could identify, and I came across a little cross roads and I circled it; did a 360. The admiral came up and said, 'Where are we?' and I said, 'Oh, sir, we're right here, admiral,' and I continued up and the next time I circled to find out where I was, I couldn't find the Atlantic Ocean! He came up again and said, 'Where are we?' And again I said, 'Right here.'

"He said, 'We're lost aren't we?' I said, 'Oh, no we're not lost I know where we are, we're right here.'

"He looked at me and he says, 'Where are your Navy wings?'

"I looked up at him and said, 'Well, I can't wear Navy wings, admiral, because I'm not a Naval aviator.'

"He thought he was in this damn situation in a Navy airplane and the guy was not a pilot! He turned white and went back and sat down. I finally found my way up there, in fact to get in to Quonset Point we had to go under the Narragansett Bay Bridge, we were tight on the deck all the way up.

"After we landed, I asked him when his departure was and he said, '1300 the next afternoon, but I'm not going back with you, I'm taking the train back. I want you to get in that airplane and I want you to taxi it back to Norfolk!'

"It was a Friday, I hadn't been in the Navy very long, and I said to myself, 'Well hell, I'm up in Quonset Point, Rhode Island, in an hour on a train I could be home in New Haven to see Norine.' So I left the airplane there but I never sent an RON [remain over night] message or any kind of movement message back to base. I went home and on Monday morning, took the train back, got in the airplane and flew back to Norfolk. When I got to Norfolk, I had in the meantime become friendly with all the line boys and mechanics, I parked my airplane and got out, the line boy said, 'Ooh, shit!'

"I said, 'What's wrong?'

"He said, 'I got orders to tell you to report to Commander Fitzgerald the minute you got on the ground.'

"So I went to Commander Fitzgerald's office and Jesus, he gave me some kind of tongue lashing like you wouldn't believe. Especially about taking the whole weekend off; they didn't know where the hell I was with that Navy airplane!

"'What did you do to the admiral, what the hell did you do to the admiral?' Fitzgerald said.

"'I didn't do anything, I told you the weather was bad, I told you we were going to have a tough time getting up there, but I got up there without crashing the damn airplane, I should get a medal for that!'

"Well, he handed me a telegram, the Navy called them speed letters, it basically said, after so much agitation, the admiral requested Bernard report immediately to Corpus Christi Naval Air Station for designation as a Naval aviator.

"Eddy and another fellow named 'Johnny' Johnson, C. A. Johnson, were included in those orders. We were given three days to travel to Corpus Christi from Norfolk. Well, Johnny had a better idea, he knew three gals, and he said, 'Why don't we get a room in the Ole' Henry hotel, in Highpoint, North Carolina, and we'll have a weekend party?' which we did."

Doesn't there seem to be a running theme with their driving trips?

"We didn't leave an awful lot of time after that weekend to drive to Texas, but we made it! Well, since we had the background of Pan Am, they decided not to put us through the entire flight syllabus, which would take about fifteen months so they gave us a one month hurry-up course. We didn't do the primary phase, only some of the intermediate phase but all of the advanced phase. The primary phase was flying M2s, the PT-17 the Army Air Corps called them. We also did some flying in the Vultee 'Vibrator' the SNV-1."

Eddy tells of some rather inventive touch-and-go techniques he and Harry performed during one of their training exercises.

"We were flying one directly behind the other when it was decided we would really get some excellent touch-and-go practice. On final approach, one of us would sing out over the radio: 'Tail wheel only' and we'd land only touching the tail wheel to the runway. Next landing it was left wheel and tail wheel only, then right wheel and tail wheel only, then left wheel only, right wheel only until all possibilities were exercised. The lone flight instructor observing the touch-and-go landings on the ground was struck with apoplexy trying to determine who was 'hot-rodding' because actually 'nuggets' [advanced student pilots] often land left wheel and tail wheel only but not deliberately."

Harry recollects another sketchy touch-and-go training mission, this time at night.

"Staying in the pattern, they put up about twenty-five airplanes to do touch-and-goes, but at night? Dog fighting with twenty-five other airplanes doing touch-and-goes? I said to myself, this is crazy. So I turned out my nav lights and I headed inland for thirty minutes. After thirty minutes I turned around headed back, turned on my nav lights and landed. Fortunately they didn't have any incidents that night.

"We completed that training and the three of us were designated Naval aviators. On the completion of that program, even though we had a lot of time in the DC-3 [R4D], they still required us to spend thirty days in Fort Worth, Texas. American Airlines had a contract to check out those Naval aviators who graduated and were going to go into the Naval Air Transport Service."

During their time at Meacham Field, in Fort Worth, Texas, they spent the entire month of June 1943 in intensive flight training and ground school. American Airlines had monthly graduation at the BOQ (Bachelor Officers Quarters) and Harry and Eddy needed dates for the evening. The two prepared themselves with their dress whites and their shoes were polished and buffed. They had the on-duty Red Cross driver haul them into Fort Worth so they could search for dates for the evening. While they sipped their fountain sodas from Renfro's drugstore, they spotted two girls sitting on a bench just outside the store. Eddy recalls one was quite attractive and the other, probably the girl's mother, wore a green hat and had her back to him. As they approached the girl and her mother, they quickly realized that the green hat wearer was indeed NOT the other's mother and Harry and Eddy were both greeted with a friendly, "Hi Y'all" smile. Coincidentally they were both named Betty Lou, and although I don't know what happened to the one they first noticed, the one wearing the green hat became Eddy's wife and they have spent fifty-three years together as of this writing and are still counting.

The story of Eddy's wedding is an interesting story in itself. Before we get back to Navy flying, let's hear Harry tell the story of Eddy's wedding or if this was an episode of Perry Mason: The case of the wedding that almost wasn't.

"After our stint in Texas we went back to VR1 in Norfolk, Virginia, and Eddy and Betty Lou corresponded for the next three years. In the meantime she went to work for Consolidated in Fort Worth making airplanes. I guess she was 'Rosy the Riveter.' In 1946 she wrote letters to Eddy saying she had a two-week vacation and she would like to come up and visit him providing Norine would write to her mother and convince her she would be well chaperoned. So Norine wrote the letter and Betty Lou stayed with us.

"Well, Eddy got so many flights out of Patuxent River NAS, we had moved to Patuxent from Norfolk, he saw very little of her in the two-week period. I was gone a lot as well so Norine entertained her. The night Betty Lou was supposed to leave, they woke us up about three in the morning and said, 'We are going to get married!' It was a very short courtship except by mail. 'Wonderful,' we said, and we got up and partied a little while."

Short courtship indeed, Eddy recalls that in total, from June 1943, when he met Betty Lou, until they were married on July 5, 1946, they had only seen each other a total of six times!

"They set their wedding date for July 5 and I was to be best man and Norine was to be matron of honor. It was going to be a Friday evening at the chapel at Patuxent River. I told Eddy he had better send out invitations if he wanted people to come to the wedding. He said, 'No, I'm not doing that, I'm going to call each one and invite them personally to my wedding.'

"On Tuesday before the wedding, he was to be married on Friday at five-o'clock with a reception to follow, I was dispatched to Argentia, Newfoundland, and Eddy was dispatched to Bermuda. My mission was simple; I was to drop off passengers and mail and parts, pick up mail, passengers and supplies and come back the next day. But I got fogged in, I mean really fogged in. I finally decided I was leaving Thursday because I had to get back and make all the arrangements for the wedding. So I had a Jeep lead me out to the runway, you couldn't see your hand in front of your face, and he lined me up on the white line. Well, I pushed those throttles forward and took off, and then it didn't matter because I couldn't see anything once I was in the air. So I got home and there was an awful lot to do, including having a stag party at my place. But with Eddy still in Bermuda Thursday night, we decided to make it a couple's party. We had a great time and we did a lot of 'Cardinal Huffing.'"

Harry demonstrates.

"Here's to Cardinal Huff, he's true blue, if he doesn't go to heaven he'll go the other way so drink chug-a-lug, drink chug-a-lug! Some of the guys were in the kitchen playing 'Ten or no count.' That is when you strip down to your waist, to get ready for battle. Then you grab a handful of chest hairs and pull. If you don't get at least ten, it's no count!

"Well, poor Betty Lou, she had never drunk before so she got sicker than hell later on. When the party was over she went in the bathroom to toss her cookies, we had one bathroom in that house, and she threw up in the bathtub. Well, about five-o'clock in the morning the phone rings and it's Eddy's two brothers driving down from Rutland, Vermont. It was July and it was so hot, there's no AC anywhere. They are plum tired and sweating and they were looking forward to a nice bath. Well, I had to wake everybody in my neighborhood in the morning looking for a damn plunger to get that bathtub cleaned out before they got there!

"Eddy in the meantime was still in Bermuda. His mission was to pick up the crew of the Naval Academy boats that were in the first Newport to Bermuda yacht race following WW II. Well, all of the sail boats got becalmed about fifty miles out to sea. He was there night after night waiting for the scenario to change."

Eddy fills in the details....

"...[There was a captain] and after dinner, we conversed as to our common problem—my pending marriage and his son who was aboard one of the yachts, the *Highland Light*. The captain was in Bermuda, on leave, to be with his son. It was decided that the captain would request a Navy tug to tow the two Navy yachts back to Bermuda because the Gulf Stream would move them north each evening when the local wind died. This was done and we departed the next day with all hands aboard."

Harry continues.

"In the meantime I had somebody get flowers for the chapel, I had to get Eddy's uniforms ready, and I had to get a ring. We ended up borrowing our friend Roger Hoys' grandmothers ring that he always wore. I'm running around getting things together and I had to postpone the wedding from five-o'clock until seven in order to give Eddy a chance to get in and get dressed. So after all the arrangements were done, I was tired so I went home and took a bath and got in my white uniform.

"About this time Eddy landed; he must have had that thing fire-walled all the way up to Patuxent NAS. Well, he had a wonderful wedding at 7:00 and a reception at the officers club.

"They were going to go to Washington for the honeymoon and everybody had had a little something to drink so he decided after the reception he would invite a handful of his best friends to his BOQ room. We didn't have any rice so we went into the galley and got boxes of puffed rice and gave everybody a box and we were throwing puffed rice all over the BOQ. We were ankle deep in puffed rice that night!

"Well, after a while Eddy insisted that we all follow him to Washington to their hotel so we could continue the party. I'm not sure how he got there; Betty Lou must have driven. Anyway we followed for a little bit and eventually dropped off, we weren't going to spoil his evening."

So concludes the saga of Eddy's wedding. It is amazing that after all that, everything went off fairly smoothly and what's more is the fact that Eddy and his lovely wife, Betty Lou, continue to live a happy life together in San Diego.

While we are on the subject of weddings and marriage, I might as well tell you about Norine. Harry met Norine at the big fall event of their college, called the freshman "P" dance, where the upperclassmen would take the incoming freshmen. I don't know who came up with this idea, but I can bet you all the fellows would have paid him thanks....

Norine was hanging around with a friend named Dickie Sexton and Harry had a good friend, Gordon Reager. Well, as it were, both the guys got the great idea to ask Dickie, the blonde (Norine had jet black hair), to the dance.

Eventually, a spinning Lincoln solved their dilemma and Harry ended up with Norine and Gordon with Dickie.

Right away they knew they would be married and so they were on August 4, 1943.

NAVY

Now back to Navy flying. Squadron VR1 at the time was located at Norfolk, Virginia. It was basically a Navy airline and had stops all up and down the east coast from Newfoundland through the eastern seaboard to Key West, Florida, then Cuba, Puerto Rico and the Panama Canal. One particular day stands out to Harry during his time in Norfolk. It happened to be Easter Sunday and what should have been a pleasant remembrance almost turned into a final farewell for Harry.

"Easter Sunday of 1943 was a terrible, terrible day at Norfolk, Virginia. With high winds of course you get high seas, which someone reported to me later were eighteen- to twenty-foot ground swells. On top of all this we had freezing rain; a very bad combination for pilots. A PB2Y4, which is a big four-engine flying boat, came up from NAS Banana River, Florida, which we now know as Cape Canaveral or Kennedy. That was the Naval air station where they did all the boat training on the east coast. They flew into Norfolk in this terrible weather, tried to land at Hampton Roads with these high swells and sunk. I was the standby duty officer on that Sunday, the duty officer got first call about the seaplane crashing in Hampton Roads and there were people lost overboard. He went out, when the alarm went off, in a Grumman Duck, the J2F, which is a single-engine biplane with a long snout underneath it. As soon as he took off, his airplane iced up and he crashed just off the end of the runway in Hampton Roads.

"The alarm went off again. I was in my dress blues, because it was Easter Sunday, and I never figured that the standby duty officer would have any problems, but the alarm went off again and at the time I was trying to get a call through to Norine, who I was going to marry that following summer. But in those days getting a long distance call through wasn't that easy and I was having problems. Well, the alarm went off again and I went down to the ready room. About this time a doctor in his bridge coat, which is a big Navy blue overcoat and a corpsman, a Navy male nurse, showed up and we got into a JRF Grumman amphibian. Normally it is a very good rough water airplane.

"When you are in rough water, the technique calls for you to land into the wind at a forty-five-degree angle to the swell. When you come up off the swell, you may be airborne but you will be stalling and you will stall and fall down the other side of the swell. That's the theory. When I took off, I wasn't more than 300 feet in the air when I saw the wing of the duty pilot's plane, the J2F, floating around in the water. Well, unbeknownst to me, the crash boats that were out there looking for the bodies earlier had already picked up Mike and the mechanic he took with him. So not knowing that, we tried to land alongside his airplane to pick him up. I used the technique, which often worked but didn't work this time, and I came off the crest of that tremendous swell and the airplane was heading straight up, shaking like a wet dog and fell off on one wing and knocked the right wing float off and half sunk the Grumman Duck. Luckily, the three of us were able to get out and get on the wing.

"At that point something happened that I thought was terrible. The doctor had taken his bridge coat off when he got on the airplane, and he ordered the corpsman to swim under the cabin to retrieve his bridge coat."

Harry's face still showed the anger he must have felt as he stood on the slippery, undulating wing of that Grumman Duck, the rain pelting them and the unmitigated gall of that lieutenant commander. He shook his head still not believing that a doctor of all people would risk the life of someone over a bridge coat.

"He was a lieutenant commander, and I was an ensign but that wouldn't have mattered because I was the pilot in command of that situation and had I known that at the time I would have countermanded his order because that was a very inhumane thing to do; send a man down underwater to get his damn coat.

"The crash boats picked us up and brought us back and for two or three weeks that airplane of mine, half sunk with one wing sticking out of the water drifted around Hampton Roads, and every time I took off I could see it, and think, 'When the hell is the Navy going to go out and sink that damn thing!'

"They never entered that accident in my logbook. They never considered that an accident because it was done under an emergency attempt air/sea rescue done under extremely adverse conditions. Years later I was in an officers club someplace and a couple of guys at the bar were talking about, 'When the Navy sunk three flying boats in the same afternoon at the same time.' I looked at them and said, 'How would you like to hear the true story from one of the pilots?'"

Among the many missions Harry took part in, one was interesting in the fact that it called for the strafing and bombing of Virginia Beach, Virginia. Really...well, sort of....

"While I was in Norfolk, I was assigned an interesting mission. The Curtiss SNC-1, which is a tandem two-seat trainer, looked very much like a Japanese Zero, if you didn't look at it too close. They painted it and camouflaged it up to make it look like a Zero and we were assigned to work with Metro Goldwyn [Mayer] camera crews off of Virginia Beach that were working with the amphibious training command from Little Creek, Virginia. They would run their landing craft in to the beach and we would strafe the beach and drop 'bombs' while the MGM crews filmed. And those film clips were in every war film MGM ever put out so if you look real close I'm that slanty eyed guy that's shooting up the place!"

It wasn't too long after this "mission" that the powers that be decided to move the squadron from Norfolk, Virginia to Patuxent River, Maryland. Harry had just come in from a flight when the skipper of the squadron, "Slim" Larned, approached him.

"'What are you doing for the rest of the day?' he said.
"'I'm going home and go to bed.'
"'Oh, come on I'm looking for a copilot. We have moved the squadron up to Patuxent River, Maryland, and I want to go up and look from the air to see where the best places are to live.'
"I said, 'That's a good idea!'

"Well hell, there wasn't any place to live. The only places to live were little farmhouses. There was a row of beautiful homes, including Mary Pickford's [the silent film actress] home, which became the quarters for the commanding officer of the overseas air station. There were some homes on the Chesapeake Bay along what they called the gold coast and also on the west shore of the Patuxent River for well-to-do people from Washington. So we were not successful on finding the best place to live."

Even though the trip wasn't a complete success, Harry and Norine eventually found reasonable accommodations and began to adjust to living in Maryland. In the general vicinity of where they lived were several rather exquisite homes, which were owned by wealthy businessmen, politicians and even the owner of National Breweries in Baltimore, Maryland. One particular house stood out in Harry's memory, named Mulberry Fields.

"It had the most beautiful formal gardens with peacocks strolling around in it. A retired Marine colonel owned it by the name of William Garland Fay. They used to have pretty big parties there with a lot of notables down from Washington. We were invited to one of their garden parties and Admiral Landes, who was a Navy admiral but was in charge of the Merchant Marines during the war, engaged my wife Norine in conversation. There were several people sitting around drinking cocktails or whatever and he asks Norine, 'What class was your husband?'

"These were all ring knockers, as whenever they had the opportunity they would knock their academy rings.

"Norine said, 'Well, he didn't graduate from the Naval Academy, he is only a reserve officer.'

"That admiral got all over her and said, 'Don't you ever say ONLY, the reserves are what win the war, all the regular Annapolis people do is keep the cannons shined!'"

Harry laughed uproariously.

"Well, we sat in those gardens, and the house was about a mile from the Patuxent River. The house was up on a hill, then there were terraced gardens down to a level field that ran out to the river and if you sat on the gardens and looked out at the river, there was a row of trees that ran to the river that were perfectly parallel to each other all the way to the river. It was gorgeous; the peacocks would stroll around just absolutely beautiful. That was our touch of rich living during WW II."

Once things got settled in at the new Naval air station, a new set of orders came to fruition that had the pilots of Squadron VR1 flying the North Atlantic route. They had received new DC-4s (R5Ds) right off the Douglas assembly line and the flight crews were, in Harry's words, "delighted to get the two extra engines." They wound up with twelve DC-4s, not a bad arsenal for the first transport squadron ever, but with the Navy's budget I suppose they could afford to have the best. The squadron was filled with vice presidents and executive officers from most of the major airlines at the time, Braniff, Northeast, TWA, United, American and it just so happened that two pilots from Pan Am named Harry Bernard and his friend Eddy Frankiewicz were in the mix.

The crews were based in Patuxent River, Maryland, and flew ten flights a week to Stephenville, Newfoundland, the Azores, which for all practical purposes is just east of nowhere but more specifically about 1,000 miles west of Lisbon, Portugal. Some flights would go to Port Lyautey, French Morocco, and others went to Prestwick, Scotland. When Paris was liberated all of the flights would then fly into Paris. In all it was a tough trip being about fifty hours round trip, which is amazing because I made the trip in seven or so hours on a recent visit to Sweden. I wondered exactly how the pilots navigated across the big pond and Harry was glad to give me a short lesson on navigation.

"Most of our navigation was celestial navigation. In the daytime, we used a drift meter, which was a periscope sight that looked down through the belly of the aircraft and you lined up the grids with the direction of the waves. The waves will tell you which direction the wind was blowing; you could use that to judge the strength and direction of the wind. When the wind was blowing, the whitecaps would fall with the wind so you knew the wind was coming from the opposite direction.

So you line up the grids and compare it with the heading you had on the airplane and that told you how much crab you had, so you could correct for wind drift. In the daytime we could use the sextant and take positions from the moon if it was out and the sun.

"We also had Loran which is not the Loran we have now, Loran C, this was the original Loran, I think it was called Loran A. And it was a fairly precise method of navigation, but we didn't have enough Loran stations to give us complete coverage on the North Atlantic. When you were upgraded to pilot in command, you had to navigate one trip first using celestial navigation. So you had to become very proficient in that. We used the sextant to take lines of position on the twenty-six navigational stars, plus the sun and moon, if they were visible. If you did it very accurately, you worked a triangle, three lines of position and where they intersected was always a triangle. That triangle was about ten miles on a side and if you put a dot in the middle of that triangle, that was your current position, that was basically how we got across the North Atlantic. I remember one of our navigators, we were off the coast of Greenland, I heard him say 'Whoa, come here!' and he had a very accurate navigational triangle off the sun, the moon and our line of position which was very unusual. That was the best navigator I ever had, John Childs, he later became vice president of Irving Trust Company on Wall Street; he was a big banker.

"He was also an avid outdoorsman, he fished and hunted all over the place, then he would write articles about it and it would be published in *Field & Stream*. We had a trailing antenna on our airplanes, which we would let out several hundred feet for communication purposes. I often accused him of dropping a line in the Saint George's Bay and trolling for fish on the way into the airport! I shot quail with him in the Azores and I went fishing with him one time in Newfoundland. We met a fellow named Lee Wulff, he was a good friend of John's. At that time he was writing for *Field & Stream*, he had not become editor yet. He was working for the Newfoundland government in its tourism department; it was an effort to promote Newfoundland as a destination for tourists. He had a PBY [amphibious plane] for his own use and he would fly into big lakes and so forth and make movies of fishing and use them for promotional purposes. We went fishing at Harry's River and I said, 'How did they know I was coming?'

"We fished there and we weren't doing too well. Well, Lee would reach into his vest and hat and pull out hooks and feathers and linen thread, and he would look at the bugs that were floating on the surface of the water and then tie a fly to duplicate what that bug looked like. And he caught a fish, fifteen or sixteen pounds; a good-sized fish. I learned more in that one day of fishing with Lee Wulff than I did the rest of my life! He was a wonderful person."

It is interesting to note that when Harry first told me the story of fishing with Lee Wulff, it was the Christmas prior to my moving to North Carolina to tape him for this book. We were sitting in the living room of my family's farm in Virginia listening intently to Harry when he pops out the name Lee Wulff. Well, my brother was sitting beside me and I looked at him and he looked at me and we both simply shook our heads, amazed at the casualness of his mentioning a personal fishing trip with one of the greatest fly fishermen in the world.

"At the end of each leg across the North Atlantic, we would lay over at that airport for twenty-four hours, then we would catch the next flight in for the next leg. Well, the next day after that fishing I picked up my flight back to Washington, D.C., with a load of passengers. We did not allow smoking in the cabin because we had three cabin tanks that held 474 gallons of fuel each; so there were a lot of fumes in the compartment. This fellow comes up on the flight deck to see how we operated. I got to talking to him and had a cup of coffee and he asked me if I ever went fishing in Newfoundland. I said I'd only done it once and it was yesterday, and I told him the story about fishing with Lee Wulff. Well, he knew Lee Wulff and his work and used a lot of his flies and he said some of the best fishing streams in the world are in Newfoundland. They may not be as good as some of the fishing streams in Russia and he said some of the streams in Italy are very good as well. He was talking about all the wonderful streams around the world I said, 'Have you fished all of those?'

"He said, 'Yes.'

"I said, 'Well, what do you do for a living, you must travel around a lot.'

"He said, 'Yes, I do travel around a lot, I work for the State Department.'

"Well, we chatted some more and then he went back to the cabin. Soon after, my radio op got a message from Washington: 'Is Admiral William C. Bullet aboard?' So I went back and talked to the orderly and asked if we had a William C. Bullet aboard. He said they did and said, 'It's that fellow over there.'

"It was the one I had just been talking to about fishing around the world. I went over to him and said I have a radio message from Washington and they wanted to know if you are on board. He said, 'Well, tell them, no!' he said, 'They want to give me a big reception there and I don't want a reception, I just want to get off the damn airplane and go home!'

"I wired back, 'Negative, he's not on board.'

"Well, the next day when I got back to the base in Patuxent River, they were waiting for me, and they threw the book at me. They threatened to court martial me, and finally when I explained that I was only conceding to his wishes, that he did not want a big military reception, the skipper finally cooled down and understood, but he did threaten to court martial me."

Communication over the North Atlantic was almost as primitive as the navigation. It seemed like transmissions were cut off or interrupted by just about anything including sun flares, bad weather or whether or not the radios felt like working on a particular day.

"Our communications operated in high frequency spectrum, 4, 5, or 6 kilohertz. I had a flight from Prestwick, Scotland, and flew off the south coast of Greenland in the wee hours of the morning. I guess acting out of boredom I called Point Christian, which is the southern tip of Greenland. I made contact and started to chat with the radio operator, I asked a lot of questions about their lifestyle, they very seldom went outside because it was so cold and they had so much snow. So they spend their tour of duty inside, and I said, 'What do you eat?' He said one word: 'SPAM!' Every which way, fried, baked, sautéed, everything. With that an operator in North Africa, at Port Lyautey, Morocco, came on and said, 'I'll tell you what, we eat a lot of SPAM over here too!' Well, the radio operators all around the Atlantic rim were talking about their diets and most of them were eating SPAM! As far as South America, the southern part of Africa, the Canadian perimeter of the Atlantic, Iceland, Greenland everybody was eating SPAM. We chatted about half an hour about eating SPAM and how we made a half-hour conversation about SPAM, I don't know, but we did!

"The radio reception that night was outstanding, which was amazing, because it was on that same flight between Greenland and Goose Bay, Labrador, that I saw the greatest display of the aurora borealis I have ever seen in the North Atlantic. We could see it often, but this was fantastic! It was like searchlights flooding the sky. It was amazing because normally when you had that kind of display, the reception would be affected, but it wasn't on that particular night."

I asked Harry if he ever carried anybody famous on his trips across the North Atlantic. He thought for a second and then "Oh" *he says.* "Did I ever tell you about the time I flew Charles Lindbergh?"

No, Harry you didn't....

"After Paris was liberated, and I'm not sure which leg it was, I think it was the first leg from Paris to the Azores. I had an orderly who was very friendly; he loved everybody type of guy. He would start a conversation with anybody about anything. I guess he didn't recognize the name Charles A. Lindbergh on the passenger manifest. Lindbergh was sitting in his seat, and this steward sat next to him and engaged him in conversation. Then he asks Lindbergh, 'Is this the first time you have flown the North Atlantic?' And to Lindbergh's credit he didn't say, 'Are you kidding son, do you know who the hell I am?' He just looked at the steward and simply said 'No.' As a result, when

Lindbergh wrote his book, *The Wartime Diaries of Charles A. Lindbergh*, it cost me $29.95 to look for my name in that diary. Every time he flew with an Army Air Corps person, that guy's name, rank, serial number, and hometown would be in the diary. When it came time for his flight back from Paris he said 'A Navy crew' carried me back!"

Harry laughed and shook his head. "Another missed chance at my fifteen minutes of fame," *he added.*

Speaking of a liberated Paris, Harry tells a story of when he was there just after the liberation. They had ten trips a week there and Harry usually had a forty-eight-hour layover. In this time Harry would take a jeep and wander the countryside, visiting the cathedrals and generally taking in all there was to see. On his layover just after the liberation, Harry describes the town as having "gone berserk ... there were people everywhere."

He was standing on the corner of the Royal Monceau hotel smoking a pipe, "watching all the girls go by" *he said, when a French girl came out of nowhere and threw her arms around him and introduced herself rather presumptively. Harry, not being allergic to such a thing, told her,* "Hold on a minute honey, let me get rid of this pipe," *and stuffed the lighted pipe in his pocket. He continued to celebrate the liberation with her and the next thing he knew, he felt a burn on his leg and looked down to see his pipe fall onto the sidewalk. Disheveled, Harry bent down to pick up his pipe only to rise in the face of an anonymous Frenchmen who exclaimed,* "Oh, monsieur, you have just kissed half of Paris!" *Well, I suppose the French lass had done some celebrating of her own, even before the liberation.*

The next stories are little quips that Harry remembered during other conversations, mostly about the DC-4s and experiences with them, especially in bad weather. They all took place sometime between 1943 and about 1945 but as Harry says, "things get a little hazy that far back."

"The aircraft we flew, the Douglas DC-4s, most of them had three cabin tanks of fuel that held approximately 474 gallons each. Well, squadron policy was to burn all four engines down to fifty gallons in each tank, then burn two engines down to twenty-five gallons and if you needed the last twenty-five gallons, just burn one engine with those twenty-five gallons. All four engines operated down to the fifty gallon level and the tanks had glass sight gauges so you could calibrate it and tell how many gallons remained in the tanks, the plane burned about 200 gallons per hour.

"One night I went back to brush up on my sextant technique and take some star shots. The navigator sat in the pilot's seat and of course the copilot sat in his seat. I was in the navigator's seat working out some positions and I needed another star shot so I got up on the navigator's stool, which is about as high as a barstool. I hung my sextant and was taking another star shot on one of the twenty-six navigational stars when the plane captain, who was responsible for fuel management reports, came back and told me there were about seventy-five gallons remaining. I said 'fine' and let me know when it gets to fifty gallons. He had just told me there was seventy-five gallons left, when all four engines quit. It was like you were driving a big truck down the road and slammed the brakes. It threw me off the stool; the deceleration was so rapid. Of course it's night, everything is dark; the only light was from the instrument panel. I ran up quickly to the cockpit to switch the fuel selector valves from the cabin tank readings to the wing tanks. You have cross feed, mixture control levers, fuel booster pumps, so I'm pulling levers and the navigator is pulling levers and the copilot is pulling levers, everyone is pulling levers! We finally got two engines on one side started, but we couldn't get the other engines started. We lost about 5,000 feet of altitude, and we were only cruising at 8,000 feet, before we could get all engines running again and sucking fuel from the tanks that they were supposed to be getting fuel from. It was a very hair-raising experience! Not only for me but also for everyone on that damned airplane, to be out in the middle of the Atlantic Ocean at four in the morning and have all the engines quit!

"As a result of that incident, which I wrote up, we decided that the fuel gauges were not accurate enough to burn all four engines down to fifty gallons, so the policy was changed to burn four engines down to one hundred, two engines down to fifty and burn one engine on the rest of those fifty gallons."

"Another little incident I had concerning the cabin tanks; you couldn't smoke in the airplane except for the flight deck. So we would let the passengers come up one at a time and let them have a smoke. At that time we were carrying several Russian pilots to Stephenville, Newfoundland, then they would catch the next leg down to Patuxent River, Maryland, and catch a shuttle to Elizabeth City, North Carolina, where they picked up PBYs that were given to Russia as our ally in WW II. A PBY is a twin engine flying boat with wheels; it is really an amphibian. They would ferry them from Elizabeth City over to Russia. On this flight, I had to go back to the cabin to use the head and as I walked through the fuel compartment, which is full of fuel vapors, there is one of the Russian pilots smoking a cigarette leaning against the gas tank! Well, I blew my cork and gave him hell and told him 'Fire, fire!' And he said, 'No fire, no fire, cigarette! No fire!' I took that cigarette and crushed it out on the palm of his hand and said, 'Fire! Fire!'

"Those Russian pilots were something else. They picked up those PBYs and I don't believe they got above 1,000 feet all the way over to Russia. In fact, one time we were making an approach into Stephenville and the ILS [instrument landing system] approach is over St. George's Bay, and I broke out about 400 or 500 feet and here is a damned PBY flown by one of those Russian pilots, right in front of me; I almost ran into him!

"There were lots of incidents like that with the Russian pilots. Even in the days when we delivered DC-3s to the Russians, when I was with Pan Am, we would fly the DC-3s up to Tehran in Iran. It was winter and it could get very cold up there and the first thing the Russians did was take off the propeller spinners and put on their own propeller spinners that had three slots in it. They would then back a truck up to the airplane; the truck had a diesel engine with a shaft coming out of it with three tines on it. They would lock those tines on the dome and kick over the diesel engine and those DC-3s would bounce on both wheels as they tried to get those engines started.

"They always started them but they never ran them up. We always preheated the engines in that cold weather, but not the Russians, they would get them started, and never do a run up or anything and they would just take off and disappear off the end of the runway. I never knew what the fatality rates were with those flights but it had to be high with that kind of flying."

"I did have a terrible problem myself one night going from the Azores to Paris. You got your heaviest weather on that route off the coast of France; we entered France at Brest. We were coming into Brest and ran into a hellacious thunderstorm, it was night of course, they always are! Daytime you can sometimes avoid them and fly around them. I had a load of Navy nurses on board and we fought that airplane trying to keep it straight and level. We were up and down four or five thousand feet in these vertical drafts, microbursts they call them now. The next thing I know, we are flat on our back, a four-engine airplane loaded with people at 9,000 feet. I had to act like an acrobatic pilot to get out of it. We got to Paris without further incident but I bet those Navy nurses had a hell of a time! We had passed the order to put on seatbelts so there were no injuries, but they had a hell of a rough ride.

"That happened once in a while on the Atlantic, not very often but when it happened it seemed to be rather severe. There was another incident, while I was on a trip from Stephenville to the Azores, also known as point 'X.' I was about a half hour behind another DC-4 flown by an American Overseas Airline crew. I didn't run into too much trouble, I had a little turbulence now and then and I landed without any real problems. But as it turned out, I talked to the pilot later and he went through what he thought was a towering cumulus and it was so turbulent inside, he lost control of the airplane. He overstressed the airplane pulling it out and was able to land OK, but that DC-4 never flew again. It sat there for the rest of the time I flew the North Atlantic to remind us to stay out of heavy weather.

All four engines had dropped about two feet on their engine mounts and every rivet on that airplane had popped. Both wing root fairings, which were maybe four or five feet wide, had come off and had gone back and cut off about a foot and a half of the horizontal stabilizer and the rudder. How he managed to get that airplane down I will never know; it was an airplane with a broken back. The interesting thing was he was on a military mission from Yugoslavia, which included Secretary General Tito from Yugoslavia. He had a very, very close call."

The North Atlantic provided Harry with many interesting and rather dangerous flights. As you can imagine, flying over the North Atlantic would sometimes result in very cold temperatures and when the weather turned bad, severe icing could result. One such incident sticks out in Harry's mind.

"I was on a trip back to Washington, D.C., The Navy flew from Stephenville then to Sydney, which is on the northeast end of Nova Scotia, then to Halifax. Sometimes we landed at Yarmouth, which is on the southwest corner of Nova Scotia and into Boston that way. The weather brief from the aerographer, which is an Army Air Corps specialist, told us that if we went over Nova Scotia we would be running into severe icing conditions. There was a cold front occlusion that was moving eastward and it would be right over Nova Scotia and we would be in it paralleling it and we would get severe icing. So he suggested we go the route everybody else was going; inland. We headed inland and we were coming down past Presque Isle, Maine, when we started to pick up severe icing. As it turned out, that cold front occlusion had stalled right over the coast of Maine instead of moving off the coast of Nova Scotia and we were in this severe icing condition all the way.

"Our airplanes were modified, they originally had ten gallons of propeller deicing fluid, but we put in fifty gallons of deicing fluid. The deicing fluid couldn't handle the weather, of course if you can't deice the propeller blades, those are airfoils and it starts to affect your efficiency. We were losing airspeed and of course the airframe was picking up ice, the whole airplane was icing over. There was nothing we could do to improve the situation. I called Boston and I told them we had a severe icing emergency and I was letting out to sea to ditch; I couldn't stay in the air. My air speed was down below 100 knots and we normally flew 170 knots and I had a load of passengers and it was about three in the morning. I got out in the ocean, so I wasn't worried about running into Mount Katahdin or other mountains up there in New England and let down over the ocean. We had radar altimeters so we knew exactly how high we were above the water.

"There is a weather phenomenon called ocean temperature inversions, and when you get down a few hundred feet of the ocean it is much warmer than the air. So you get a warming effect from the ocean even though the water may be fifty degrees, the air might be twenty degrees so it is comparatively warm.

"I gave them my ditching position, and about that time a hunk of ice came off of one of the propeller blades. When that comes off, it is like a cannon shot when it hits; it's a loud noise. Now all the propellers are shedding ice and becoming more efficient and we are picking up a little airspeed so I cancelled my ditching position and told them I believe I can make it into Boston. So I got into Boston, and I kid you not, I had eight to ten inches of heavy rime ice all over my airplane, everything, prop spinners, antennas, windshield, I actually had to open the side window and look out to land the airplane."

I can only imagine what went through those passengers' heads when they realized they were heading out to sea to ditch. And I am sure when that ice flew off the props and hit the plane; there were more than a few prayers and crossings going on.

Ice wasn't the only weather problem Harry and the other pilots had to contend with. Severe winds and storms often plagued the pilots as a story about landing in the Azores demonstrates.

"I remember one time getting caught in what I think was a hurricane. The weather reporting was very primitive, we didn't have satellites and even communication was primitive. I got caught going into the Azores. The city was, well we called it Lagens and we didn't find out until after the war that it was Lages with no 'n.' I got caught in this weather and the only approach was an automatic direction finder off of a non-directional beacon. The airport was situated in a valley between two high mountains and the runway was very close to a cliff, possibly 200 feet high that protects that island from the Atlantic storms.

"When I did get a hold of Lages, they told me the wind was directly across the runway at seventy knots. Well, normally the maximum crosswind allowable is about twenty knots and to boot it was a steel mat runway. A steel mat runway is made up of a series of perforated steel sheets that lock like tongue and groove wood. Well, when I hit that runway I couldn't believe the crab angle I had to maintain to keep lined up with that runway. Even on a normal landing, under normal conditions, ten knots of wind right down the runway is ideal, when you hit that mat, it is so rough; it feels like the landing gear is going to punch right up through the wings. Just exaggerate that by many times and you get the idea of the feeling of hitting that runway in those conditions. I wound up going down that steel runway, which of course was wet, sideways. That was the first time I landed an airplane sideways. I was very happy to finally get down because the closest alternate airport, was Craw field in French Morocco, which is four hours from the Azores in that DC-4."

Not all of Harry's trips were death defying and exciting. Some were downright heartbreaking. In modern times, the thought of downing an airliner in the frigid waters of the North Atlantic are horrifying. Imagine if you will, that you are an observer, looking down into a scene of a crash, in which people were dying and you could do nothing about it. I had never heard this story and I would have never asked Harry to relive those hours above the North Atlantic but I suppose he felt as though the story had to be told. This was, however, his biography, and to not include such an event would perhaps not give you an idea of the type of man Harry is.

He sat quiet in his chair and smoothed his mustache. His eyes looked forward purposefully and I could see he wanted to say something perhaps uncomfortable. His eyes stared straight ahead and with his voice low and soft and without turning his head toward me he began his story....

"July 1945 I got my briefing in the Azores. I got my weather folder, my navigational charts and I was told by the briefing officer that a B-17 had ditched at sea with nineteen people on board.

"I said, 'Nineteen people on a B-17?'

"Well, the war was over in Europe and they were using the bombers and loading them with people, not too many, but maybe twice what their normal crew was.

"One engine had caught fire, this was about ten the night before I left, and they had ditched in the sea and had given their ditching position. We were told to be on the lookout for any signs of survival of any kind. When I took off from the Azores, I had a load of people, and I made an announcement, we didn't have a PA system, but I went back in the cabin and I announced that a B-17 had ditched at sea about 135 miles northwest of the Azores and I would like them to keep a sharp eye out if they see any debris or anything that might indicate where the plane hit the water. We had a thirteen and a half hour flight plan from the Azores to Stephenville; we had pretty good head winds. We had just about leveled out at our cruising altitude; it was one of those beautiful mornings in the Azores about 10:00 A.M., twelve hours after the ditching. There were just a few scattered cumulus clouds otherwise a beautiful flying day. My copilot was Bernie Young and I said to Bernie, 'Well, I don't think we stand much chance at 8,000 feet of spotting anything in the water.'

"It is amazing how hard it is to spot anything even from a much lower altitude. We were now on a northwesterly heading and I am looking to my left, which would make it a southwesterly heading, I thought I saw something in the water.

"I said to Bernie, 'What do you make of that, is that an oil slick?'

"We had binoculars; this was about ten or twelve miles south of our track. He said, 'No, I think that is just the sun reflecting off the water.'

"I said, 'Yeah, I guess you're right.'

"We didn't want to let down to a lower altitude because it was a thirteen and a half hour flight and we would not have had enough fuel to climb back up to our cruising altitude and back to Stephenville, Newfoundland.

"I don't know what caused me to do this, but as we headed on track I kept looking down at that spot until I was bent over and looking under the wing and I saw the dye marker. This is about forty miles from where they reported their ditching position and they had several airplanes out there looking, the Army Air Corps aircraft, and some RAF aircraft. They had two B-17s which were air/sea rescue B-17s. Under the B-17s they had a big life raft and the life raft had six spring-loaded lines and when you dropped that life raft in the water the impact with the water would release those lines and they went out several hundred feet.

"When I saw this dye marker, my heart nearly flipped over in my chest. I can't describe the feeling that I had."

Harry sat back in his chair after demonstrating how he looked under the wing of that DC-4. He was visibly upset and his voice quivered as he described what he saw.

"They had been in that water twelve hours or more, probably dead except for the one who pulled the dye marker. I reduced power on all four engines and went into a steep bank and dove on the spot. When I got down about 300 feet, I reported five men in a life raft. It turned out later that they were not in a life raft; there were five crew members with arms locked in their Mae West's, which made them look like they were in a life raft. Even at 300 feet, I couldn't tell that they were in the water.

"I gave the position and about the time I gave the position, a Pan Am Constellation from Bermuda to the Azores interrupted and said, 'Your position is about forty miles in error.'

"I said, 'Negative, your position is forty miles in error, the position I gave is the proper position!'

"They were listening to this conversation in the Azores and as it turned out there was a Navy admiral and an Army general listening. The Navy admiral was senior to the Army general and he designated me the search coordinator for the mission. I made an open announcement on the search frequency and ordered the B-17s and other airplanes down. I assigned different altitudes for each airplane, I didn't want them circling and running into each other. One of the planes was a weather observation B-25 operating out of the Azores.

"I had passed a destroyer steaming out of the Azores and I gave the B-25 that position and told him to lead the destroyer to the site. That took three hours. In the meantime, the B-17 came over and dropped the life boat, they did a beautiful job, almost hit them, it was a beautiful job; the lines went out.

"About that time one of the men died and was cut loose. So there were four survivors. It turned out the fifth man that had died was the pilot in command of the B-17. Of the four survivors, only two of them had enough strength to get to one of the lines. Only one of them had enough strength to pull himself to the lifeboat but he didn't have enough strength to climb into the lifeboat. He was hanging on the line on the side of the lifeboat.

"Three hours after the initial contact the destroyer got there. We left the Azores at about ten, we spotted them around eleven and they were picked up at two in the afternoon, which meant it was sixteen hours after the ditching. After they were picked up, we called off the search, because it was successful. I returned to the Azores after climbing out for an hour and circling for three hours while they were picked up and returning took another hour. I refueled, took off and flew the thirteen and a half hours to Stephenville. That was eighteen and a half hours in the air that day.

"The general wrote up a stunning report to recommend the highest peacetime award, the admiral overruled him and said, 'This is something all our officers do in the course of duty.' But the admiral was overruled when it got to the Pentagon for endorsement so I did wind up with the Commendation Medal and so did Bernie Young. Of the four or five thousand Naval Air Transport Service pilots, I think we were the only two to get a medal.

"I stopped at the hospital on the next trip eastbound about a week later and all the survivors were still in the hospital. They were all near death because of hypothermia. One of the survivors was the copilot and I asked him exactly what happened. He said that the outboard engine had caught fire at 10:00 P.M.; they called in their ditching position and dove for the water to try to get it to the water as quickly as possible and the altimeter read 200 feet when they hit the water. They didn't have a chance to flare or to slow down so of the nineteen people on that airplane, eleven were killed on impact. That was a very soul-wrenching experience."

It was fifty-five years after that event and it still upset Harry to tell that story. He related that the helplessness he felt being in the air and that crew being in the water was almost overwhelming. It was very quiet for a few minutes after he spoke. I couldn't think of a thing to say that would ease his still-lingering sorrow for that crew. He sat, shaking his head, still seeing the crew, bound arm in arm in their life vests clinging to life. When one expired on the way to the lifeboat I am positive if that DC-4 had pontoons he would have landed on the water and pulled them to safety himself. He took a deep breath and in typical Harry fashion, told an interesting side note to the story.

"There is one postscript to that story. I grew up with a kid in New Haven named Ray Delusa; he was one of my closest friends there. After the war we had a little party and we were reminiscing about the war. Raymond was advisor to the Yale Art School and he was on the staff of the American Museum of Natural History in New York. He went in to the military as a camouflage officer.

"He told me, 'The only exciting thing that happened to me during the whole damn war, was they had a B-17 ditch in the ocean and our ship had to change course and go down and search for it.'

"I said, 'Raymond, I'll give you all the details!'"

That indeed was a painful memory for Harry to recount, but I felt he wanted to tell it and after hearing it I'm glad he did. I hesitate to use the word "cathartic" but it seemed to lighten his load a bit and brought me right to that time and place.

On to other stories.... Just as there were celebrations for the inaugural flight across the North Atlantic, for VR1, there was a lot of hubbub about the 1,000th crossing. That flight, rather than being a single crew the whole way across, gave several crews the opportunity to take part in that historic flight. However when the opportunity came knocking for Harry, someone else opened the door....

"In 1945, squadron VR1 was flying about ten trips a week to Europe, into Port Lyautey, Morocco, and Prestwick, Scotland, until Paris was liberated in 1945. The standard procedure for utilizing crews was by flying Europe to the Azores, which was about an eight-hour flight. Layover for twenty-four hours while the previous crew that came in the day before took the next leg to Stephenville, Newfoundland; that could be as long as thirteen hours depending on the winds. The crew laying over in Stephenville would fly the last leg to the States. Usually down to Patuxent River, Maryland, or Washington, D.C..

"On the last leg after laying over in Stephenville, I was scheduled to take this trip to Washington National Airport. One of the airplane commanders came to me and said, 'My father has died, I need to get back as quickly as possible, how about if I take your flight out and you take my flight out?'

"Well, I'm a softhearted guy and that was all right with me so we swapped trips. It wasn't until after I landed in Patuxent River, Maryland, that I found that the trip I was scheduled to take out was the 1,000th crossing of the North Atlantic and Boswell had found out about it and conned me into letting him fly it! It was Naval aviation history and Boswell stole my glory!"

Harry laughed heartily and took forty years off his age. Incidentally, Harry holds no grudges against Boswell; Harry is simply not that type of man. There are more examples to come that show Harry to be just the opposite. Incidentally, Harry's good buddy Eddy Frankiewicz was plane commander of that R5D on the Paris to Azores leg.

Toward the end of 1945, Harry was sent from the east coast to squadron VR11 in Honolulu, Hawaii. The operation here was to bring back American prisoners of war. It was called RAMP, The Repatriation of American Military Prisoners. This was a very difficult period of time for Harry as he continues with the mission and then tells of his own medical emergency.

"We flew into all the islands where the Japanese had prison camps, loaded these prisoners and carried them back to Naval Air Station Oakland. That was a very heart wrenching time to see those people, some of them weighing seventy and eighty pounds and had to be carried. We did that operation for four months. That squadron was the largest of the Naval air transport squadrons; we had 1,500 pilots in that squadron. It was bigger than any airline at the time. It was a major program because there were tens of thousands of prisoners in Japanese prison camps during WW II. All of them were very badly mistreated, psychiatric cases; those were the worse kind. They always had a nurse to accompany them to keep them under control. They had guys that would continually masturbate, terrible cases.

"Some of them of course survived and came out stronger than ever. People like Senator John McCain who spent almost six years in a POW camp in Vietnam has gone on to do great things.

"When that was over, I was going to get out of the Navy and I told Norine, who was pregnant with our daughter Susan, I would be back Sunday at the latest, having left Friday night.

"Flying out to Honolulu, which was about a twelve- or thirteen-hour flight, at five or six in the morning the stewardess came up and wanted to know if I wanted breakfast and I said that would be fine. So she fixed me breakfast. We had an electric stove on board and we also had TV dinners you might call them and they were cooked in what we called radar ovens, now they call them microwaves. She didn't use the pre-prepared meals she cooked me breakfast herself. About an hour later I'm in extreme pain. We had two bunks on the flight deck of that airplane and I laid down on the lower bunk, man I was in pain but I eventually had to get up and land the plane. Well, I don't believe I could have written my name but I got up and landed the airplane and I immediately went up to BOQ and started looking around for some Sal Hepatica or something but I couldn't find anything. So I walked over to ships service and they were closed but because it was field day, they were cleaning up. I went to the dispensary and asked the pharmacist for Sal Hepatica.

"He said, 'What do you want it for?'

"I said, 'I got the sorest gut you've ever seen, I'm in extreme pain!'

"I was almost to the point of losing consciousness.

"He said, 'Well I can't give you any without a doctor's prescription.'

"I said, 'Just give me some Sal Hepatica, that doesn't require a doctor's prescription!'

"'Yes it does,' he said.

"Well, the doctor saw me and said, 'I want you in the hospital right now!'

"I said, 'OK but let me go back and take a shower I'm stinking!'

"He said, 'No you're going to the bed right now!'

"So I went to bed and he gave me some paregoric acid, he said I had gastroenteritis. That was Saturday morning, by the end of the day I was screaming. I was actually screaming and they put a corpsman on me to keep me from thrashing. The doctor made his rounds the next morning and said, 'I understand you had a bad night.'

"I said, 'If I could get out of bed I would strangle your guts!'

"He said, 'To tell you the truth I don't know what is wrong with you.'

"He was brand new, just out of medical school, a lieutenant (jg).

"He said, 'I'm sending you over to Pearl Harbor Naval Hospital.'

"And I'll never forget this; the ambulance backed up to the loading dock and this old lieutenant commander nurse, she must have been in the Navy a hell of a long while, yelled out, 'My God, this man has got a ruptured appendix, call Dr. Dorell!'

"She looked at me and knew I had a ruptured appendix and that goddamned doctor just gave me paregoric acid! So they took my appendix out and that was Sunday morning. I was out most of Sunday but the next morning I got up and took a shower; I needed a shower bad. Dr. Dorell came back in and said, 'How the hell did that bandage get wet?'

"I said, 'Well, how the hell can you take a shower without getting the bandage wet?'

"He said, 'Don't tell me you took a shower, goddamn, that water is full of bacteria you could get a bad infection!'

"He gave me hell, but it worked out all right. I'm still here!

"So I decided I had better let Norine know I wasn't going to be home Sunday at the latest. I wrote her a quick letter and shipped it off. The return address was 'Naval Hospital, Pearl Harbor.' In the meantime she was asking every crew that came back, 'When is Harry coming back? Have you seen Harry?'

"Nobody had seen me because I was in the hospital, they had to clear me first from the dispensary, they called it, and then the hospital. She got the feeling they were trying to hide something from her, like I crashed or was lost at sea or something. When she got the letter with the return address, 'Naval Hospital,' she passed out.

"When I was able to travel I came back on an aircraft carrier, the skipper of that ship said it was the roughest trip he had ever made. Eight days we spent being tossed around by a terrific storm crossing the Pacific. Most everybody was sick, I had a roommate, he had the top bunk, I was senior to him and I had the bottom bunk and he was puking all over the whole room. Once I got on the ship I didn't go to my room again, it was so bad. But I never got sick then, we spent the time playing bridge in the ward room, the few of us that weren't sick, everybody else was puking their guts out on the ship.

"When we docked at Alameda, which was both a Naval air station and a surface ship dock, all the officers disembarked first and all the enlisted men were up on the flight deck, of course everybody had been overseas during the whole damn war in the Pacific. When I walked off, here comes Norine to throw her arms around me and she is seven months pregnant. Well, a cheer went up that you wouldn't believe from those white hats up on the deck. Little did they know I had been with her just a few days before."

I guess we all have our moments in the sun and hearing those cheers must have felt good for Harry, even though they may have been for a slightly different reason than appendicitis!

4
RESERVES

Shortly after the war's end, Harry applied and was accepted to the regular Navy. He was now USN instead of USNR, however this foray into the regular Navy didn't last long. Not long after all the "i's" were dotted and the "t's" were crossed, his captain, Captain Crowe, held an all hands on deck assembly whereupon he stated that the war was over and the Annapolis boys can do a hell of a lot better job than the reserve boys.

Well, as you can imagine, Harry was none too pleased to hear those words from his commanding officer; it sickened Harry. During this time of transition, there were also several personnel changes. One of the most important was the fact that the experienced mechanics had been sent home and they were left with, in Harry's words, "...new recruits and new boots that had no experience coming in to do the maintenance work; they just weren't up to the task."

In the ensuing nine months, Harry had more engine out time than at any other time he can remember. His regular Navy experience culminated in an almost fatal series of flights, one right after the other. Harry now continues the story of those three flights that ended his time as USN.

"I took a trip down to Coco Solo Naval Air Station, in the Panama Canal zone and had to shut one engine down and we had to land on three engines. They had a chief petty officer and two sailors and that was the whole damn maintenance crew. They put a stand up in front of the engine and it was obvious what the problem was; the engine was covered with oil. He said, 'The leak is coming from the rocker box cover, it's warped on the number-seven cylinder.'

"I said, 'Well, let's put a new rocker box cover on it.'

"'We don't have any,' he said.

"I said, 'Where the hell can I get one?'

"'They have them over at Franz Field.' Which is the Air Corps base on the Pacific side. So I borrowed an airplane from operations, flew over there and got a new rocker box cover and gasket and flew back. I'm up there in the stand helping them put it on and I look at the damn cylinder, the number seven cylinder, and it had a damn crack down that cylinder big enough you could push a pencil through! And this guy is putting a new rocker box cover on this cracked cylinder! Christ, you could get fire and burn up because of that crack! So that was number one.

"I had the reputation in the squadron if the weather is bad, Bernard will fly it. I always tell every body, 'I don't care what the hell the weather is, give me enough gas to get there and I'm going!' I took a trip up to Goose Bay, Labrador, and we brought up a bunch of people and a bunch of supplies, the Navy was having Operation Frostbite, they called it. It was a Nordic exercise. The seaplanes were supposed to come down and meet us at Goose Bay, Labrador, and bring in mail and people that had to go back to the States. The weather was very bad when I went in there, and the seaplanes couldn't get down. I stayed up there for three days most of the time spent in the operations office trying to get communications, but most of the communications were radio and because of atmospheric conditions, including the aurora borealis, we couldn't get communications.

"Finally we got communications from the squadron that I should return home so I got the crew together and took off. It was at night and I headed back to Patuxent River. I think it was

Harry making an impression on the nude statue at the Pan Am training school, Miami.

Pan Am training school in Miami. Dining room straight ahead, recreation room to the left and sleeping quarters to the right.

Harry during the graduation of class 42A in Miami, April 1942. To his left is Pan Am founder, Juan Trippe. (Courtesy Aviation Information Research Corporation)

Photos of Harry's crash landing on the banks of the Ubangi-Shari river in French Equatorial Africa, July 1942. (Courtesy Aviation Information Research Corporation)

FLIGHT RECORD

FROM 2/13 **19** 42

DATE	AIRCRAFT FLOWN			FLIGHT		REMARKS OR INSTRUCTOR'S SIGNATURE CERT. NO. & RATING
	MAKE AND MODEL	CERTIFICATE NUMBER	ENGINE	FROM	TO / No. PASS.	
2/13	Douglas C-53S	12011?	P.&W. 1250	ACCRA B.W.A. EAST	—	forced night landing 90 miles S.E. Ft. Lamy — 135 miles SWof

AIRCRAFT WEIGHT AND ENGINE CLASSIFICATION — AND LOG

TO 8-3 **19** 42

Class.	Class.	Class.	INSTRUMENT FLIGHT	DUAL		SOLO		Daily Total Time
				As Instructor	As Student	Day	Night	
Hrs. Min.	Hrs. Min.	MULTI-MOTORED Hrs. 14 Min. 15	Hrs. Min.	Hrs. Min.	Hrs. Min.	Hrs. 08 Min. 15	Hrs. 06 Min. 00	Hrs. 14 Min. 15

El Geneina in French Equatorial Africa in Gaz Berda area.

Harry's log book entry regarding his crash in Africa.

Harry and Norine on their wedding day, August 3, 1943.

Harry and his father shortly after the B-17 rescue August 1945.

COMMANDER UNITED STATES NAVAL FORCES
NAVY 815

CNFA/P15
Serial: 618.

Navy 815
Fleet Post Office
New York, N. Y.

30 July 1945.

From: Commander U.S. Naval Forces, Navy 815.
To: Commander in Chief U.S. Atlantic Fleet.

Subject: LIEUTENANT HARRY BERNARD, (A5)L, USNR, (247520) - RECOMMENDATION FOR AWARD.

Reference: (a) SecNav ltr. 44-1421, AS&SL, July - December 1944, page 78.

Enclosure: (A) Suggested Citation.

1. It is desired to bring to the attention of the Commander in Chief, U.S. Atlantic Fleet, the outstanding performance of duty rendered by subject officer on 5 July 1945, and to recommend that he be granted an appropriate award.

2. Early on the morning of 5 July 1945, information was received at this base that a U.S. Army B-17 airplane had been forced down at sea approximately 160 miles away. Although the air-sea rescue organization was activated at once, the missing plane had not been located by 0900, approximately seven hours after it had landed at sea and fifteen minutes prior to the time scheduled for the take-off of Flight 141/4, commanded by Lt.(jg) Bernard. Prior to take-off, Lt.(jg) Bernard was briefed regarding the crashed airplane and was advised that he might possibly see it or its survivors while enroute to his destination.

3. Instead of following the normally to be expected routine of merely keeping a bright lookout for the crashed plane or its survivors, Lt.(jg) Bernard organized his passengers in lookout teams, instructed them, assigned them search sectors, and arranged a schedule of reliefs. Approximately one hour out from the base, the survivors were sighted from Lt.(jg) Bernard's plane.

4. Following the sighting, which was immediately reported to the base, other planes then in the air were directed to the scene, as was a USN air-sea rescue PC which had been dispatched to the area. In a short while, about six or seven

- 1 -

Official Naval recognition of Harry's work during the sighting and subsequent rescue of the downed B-17 survivors which led to his receiving the Commendation Medal.

COMMANDER UNITED STATES NAVAL FORCES
NAVY 815

CNFA/P15
Serial: 618.

Navy 815
Fleet Post Office
New York, N. Y.
30 July 1945.

Subject: LIEUTENANT HARRY BERNARD, (A5)L, USNR, (247520) - RECOMMENDATION FOR AWARD.

---

airplanes of various types and organizations were in the area, and traffic control and communications threatened to become a problem. On his own initiative Lt.(jg) Bernard took charge of the situation, assigned altitudes and areas to the planes with which he could communicate, kept the base informed of developments, acted as a voice communications relay between the base, the PC, and the planes on his voice frequency, and passed instructions to the base for transmission to other planes in the vicinity. The manner in which he performed this duty for a period of about three hours was outstanding. During a large part of this time, ComNav Navy 815 listened to the voice radio traffic and took note of the fact that the way in which Lt.(jg) Bernard carried out his mission would have done credit to an aviator of years of experience in a scouting or patrol squadron. The fact that, as a U.S. Naval Aviator, he did so well was a material contribution to the good reputation of the U.S. Navy in this area where four interested Allied Services are represented.

5. As a result of the excellent service rendered by Lt.(jg) Bernard the PC was led to the survivors with practically no delay, and four men were rescued. Whether two of these men could have held out much longer is very questionable. Although an airborne lifeboat had been dropped, and two of the survivors had boarded it, they were too exhausted to get the boat underway to pick up their other two companions. The latter two men were supported only by their inflated life jackets and were too weak to swim to the boat.

6. In view of the foregoing, it is recommended that primarily in recognition of his outstanding performance of duty, and, secondarily, as an inspiration to other transport aircraft pilots, Lt.(jg) Bernard be awarded a Letter of Commendation with authority to wear the Commendation Ribbon.

The R5D-1, Bureau No. 39144 Harry flew during the spotting and rescue of downed B-17 survivors, July 1945.

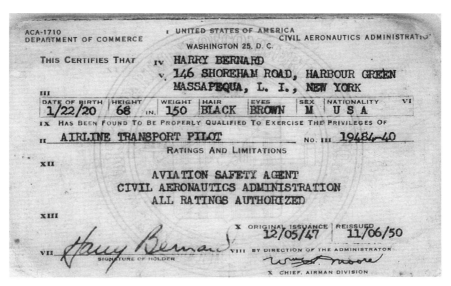

Harry's CAA license indicating his status as Airline Transport Pilot. Issued before individual type ratings were required, the CAA simply covered them all by stating, 'All Ratings Authorized.'

One of the S-55 helicopters Harry flew for the Port of New York Authority while investigating the viability of New York Airways. (Courtesy Douglas E. Olsen)

Harry as Lieutenant Commander, HS832 based at Floyd Bennett Field, New York, November 1956. This picture was taken just days before his nearly fatal crash in an S-58 while giving a check ride to a New York Airways pilot.

Front page of the *New York Daily News*, December 1, 1956 showing headline reporting the crash of Harry's helicopter during check ride. (© New York Daily News, L.P. reprinted with permission.)

At the office, Kennedy Airport, 1970.

The FAA DC-3, N6, in which Harry was involved in his last crash, April 1975. (Courtesy Ralph Pettersen)

```
FILE    DATE         LOCATION          AIRCRAFT DATA            INJURIES       FLIGHT           PILOT DATA
                                                              F  S  M/N        PURPOSE
----------------------------------------------------------------------------------------------------------------------
-0288   75/3/27  DUBOIS,PA          DOUGLAS DC-3C        CR-  0  3   0    MISCELLANEOUS    ATP,FLIGHT INSTR., AGE
        TIME - 1435                 N6                   PX-  0  1   7    OTHER PUBLIC     55, 17177 TOTAL HOURS,
                                    DAMAGE-DESTROYED     OT-  0  0   0                     3300 IN TYPE, INSTRUMENT
                                                                                           RATED.

        NAME OF AIRPORT  -  DUBOIS-JEFFERSON
        DEPARTURE POINT                       INTENDED DESTINATION               PHASE OF OPERATION
          DUBOIS,PA                             HARRISBURG,PA                      TAKEOFF: INITIAL CLIMB
        TYPE OF ACCIDENT
          COLLISION WITH GROUND/WATER: UNCONTROLLED

        PROBABLE CAUSE(S)
          PILOT-INEXPERIENCED,UNQUALIFIED PLT MADE TAKEOFF.
          COPILOT - INADEQUATE SUPERVISION OF FLIGHT
        FACTOR(S)
          PILOT IN COMMAND - EXERCISED POOR JUDGMENT
          PERSONNEL - OPERATIONAL SUPERVISORY PERSONNEL: INADEQUATE SUPERVISION OF FLIGHT CREW
          WEATHER - UNFAVORABLE WIND CONDITIONS
          MISCELLANEOUS ACTS,CONDITIONS - SEAT BELT NOT FASTENED
        WEATHER BRIEFING - BRIEFED BY FLIGHT SERVICE PERSONNEL, IN PERSON
        WEATHER FORECAST - FORECAST SUBSTANTIALLY CORRECT

        SKY CONDITION                                          CEILING AT ACCIDENT SITE
          BROKEN                                                 25000
        VISIBILITY AT ACCIDENT SITE                            PRECIPITATION AT ACCIDENT SITE
          5 OR OVER(UNLIMITED)                                   NONE
        OBSTRUCTIONS TO VISION AT ACCIDENT SITE                RELATIVE BEARING OF WIND
          NONE                                                   RIGHT CROSS WIND 068-112 DEGREES
        TEMPERATURE-F                                          WIND DIRECTION-DEGREES
          35                                                     350
        WIND VELOCITY-KNOTS                                    TYPE OF WEATHER CONDITIONS
          7                                                      VFR
        TYPE OF FLIGHT PLAN
          IFR
        FIRE AFTER IMPACT
        REMARKS- FAA REGIONAL DIR ASSUMED L SEAT.PIC STANDING.
```

NTSB report detailing Harry's crash of April 1975.

Aborted Smuggling Try At Airport, 17 Charged

By ELIZABETH G. HAMMOND

Four of the 17 men who were arrested Thursday in connection with a former C-54 military transport plane that was found carrying about six tons of marijuana that morning are free from jial on bond, including two Leland men, according to the county Sheriff's Department.

David Lloyd Brock, 38, and son David Lloyd Brock, Jr., both of Leland, Glen Edwin Biggs, 30, of Banner Elk and Bernard Latham Buey, 29 of Winston-Salem posted bond by the weekend. Bonds issued to the 17 varied from $3,500 to $115,000 depending on prior records and alleged involvement in the drug smuggling case.

The Brock men were the only two county residents arrested. Lt. John Carr Davis of the department said the drug arrests filled up the county jail, which holds 34 prisoners, for the first time in its history.

Street value of the burlap-bound bales is estimated at more than $6 million.

According to police, the plane circled the Southport-Oak Island area for about ten minutes before landing around 1 a.m. at the county airport near Yaupon Beach. Some Sheriff's Department employees noticed it on their way home

Continued on page 6

Law enforcement personnel oversee the unloading of six tons of marijuana found on a former C-54 transport plane that landed at the county airport Thursday. The bust was the fourth made in the county since the beginning of the year. More than $6 million worth of marijuana was seized; 17 people were arrested.

State Port Pilot article with photo of C-54 Harry flew from the airport at Brunswick County, North Carolina, to Wilmington, North Carolina for the DEA. (Courtesy State Port Pilot)

Harry and his trusty Piper Twin Comanche that took him wherever he wanted, circa 1998.

Harry and the author dictating this book, Bogart doesn't seem impressed.

The author, Joan and Harry celebrate the last day of dictating the book.

The author and Harry, 2001.

about eight hours and because I had been on my feet, trying to get this thing going for three days, I was just wiped out when I took off, so I went and lay down and went to sleep on the lower bunk. I told my copilot, Jim Bemis, to wake me up when we got to the states; the airport would be Presque Isle, Maine. So I'm in a sound sleep, when the flight engineer wakes me up and says, 'The airplane is on fire!'

"That was some kind of feeling waking up out of a sound sleep and being told my airplane is on fire!

"I said, 'Which engine?'

"'No,' he said, 'It's in the cabin.'

"We had no passengers and all the crew members were in the flight deck, drinking coffee. There is no reason to be back in the cabin but there was something burning back there. We couldn't find any flames so I went back to the flight deck, got in the left-hand seat and said, 'Where are we?'

"He said, 'On a west heading hitting Presque Isle in ten minutes.'

"'Is that Presque Isle?' I said, pointing in front of us.

"'Yeah that's it,' he said.

"'I don't care what the wind is, tell them to flash the lights on runway 22; I'm coming straight in!'

"We went straight in and the fire engines met us, we declared an emergency and that airplane had an emergency braking system, air brakes, I pulled them and locked the brakes. The fire engine came on and threw the ladders up, because that cabin door is quite high, maybe twelve feet in the air.

"We all piled off the airplane and the fire chief said, 'You've got some kind of an airplane burning there, you were dragging smoke all the way down.'

"They had a C-54 squadron there, which the Air Corps called 'The Snowball Squadron.' I made contact with the sergeant, who knew the airplane real well, Mckay his name was, and he said, 'I'll find out what the problem is.'

"Early the next morning, we went down there and he said, 'We give up, we can't find anything!'

"I said, 'You can't find anything, there's something burning on that damn airplane.'

"He said, 'We know that, but we can't find it.'

"I called the base operations officer, Vinny Sandberner, and said, 'Sandy, we can't find the source of the fire.'

"He said, 'Well, there is only one thing to do.'

"'What's that?'

"He said, 'Take it back up and get the fire going again!'

"I said, 'Sandy, I got three cabin tanks in there, 474 gallons each, if you think I'm going to get that burning again you're crazy!'

"He said, 'I'll come up and do it!'

"'Well, be my guest,' I said.

"While we were waiting for him to come up, we were piddling around and we were turning everything on and off and we found out where the hell the fire was. The cabin heater and the cockpit heaters were gas heaters. The gasoline is routed right over a vibrator coil that operates the heaters like an old model-T vibrator coil. It was a wooden box filled with tar with a vibrator on top of it. That fuel line had a fitting right over it and the fitting was loose and was dripping fuel on to the spark and igniting the tar, and the tar was burning and went back through the vents into the cabin. When I got back home, I went to the operations officer and said we need to do something about the routing of that fuel line for that cabin heater, there is a fitting right over that damn vibrator coil and it's a fire hazard. We did the research on it and found out that the Navy had come up with an op-nav instruction to reroute that fuel line. Well, our squadron had so few qualified personnel, that they had written it off as being accomplished but hadn't done the work; that was number two.

"The third thing that ended my Navy career up to that point was a flight I made from Bermuda back into Patuxent River, Maryland, one night; the weather was very bad. I had eleven Navy nurses on and about the time we hit the coast, I lost the number-three engine, the inboard engine on the right wing. I feathered it and shut it down. Patuxent River is about half an hour from the coast in; twenty minutes maybe. I reported in for the GCA approach, and they said we will have to get the GCA crew out you will have to hold."

A GCA approach is a Ground Controlled Approach, whereby a ground crew literally talks you down, giving you all your headings and altitude instructions. GCA minimums are 1/4 mile visibility and 100 feet of ceiling.

"I had to go into a holding pattern and hold in that damn thunderstorm, called again and they said they don't have the crew in position yet. Well, after about a half hour of this, I had had it. I particularly had it when the number-four engine went out and I had to shut it down! Here I am holding in a goddamned thunderstorm, getting tossed around like you wouldn't believe while they can't get the GCA crew out to get me down on the ground, because the weather is below limits for the low frequency range approach or any other kind of approach. The only way I was going to get in was through a GCA approach.

"I said, 'I don't give a shit about approach minimums, I'm going to make a low frequency range approach, I'm going to let down on the northeast leg and over the Chesapeake Bay, (The highest thing on the Naval air base was a water tower that was 140 feet), I am going to stay 145 feet to get below this damn weather!'

"The minimums for GCA approach were 100 feet of ceiling and 1/4 mile visibility. For the low frequency range they were 500 feet and one mile. So I made that approach over the bay, and let down and let down I was down below 200 feet when I finally made contact with the ground and I landed. This is about one-thirty in the morning. When that skipper of that squadron, Captain Crowe, got to the office that morning I was waiting to see him, and I'm doing this to him."

Harry wagged his finger and his eyebrows pinched together.

"'I've been in this goddamned squadron for four years, I'm the all-weather pilot for this squadron, I've never refused a flight if given the gas, but I have had it with you regular Navy guys, these goddamned Annapolis guys don't know shit from Shine-ola about anything!'

RESERVES

"I'm reading him the riot act and I said, 'I hereby resign my commission!'

"Of course you can't really do that but they gave me a set of orders that released me to inactive duty and put me back to reserve status. But that was one, two, three trips in a row and I had had it!"

Harry then reverted back to reserve duty; he wanted nothing whatsoever to do with the regular Navy. Three flights that nearly cost him his life were more than Harry could take. He had found his niche in the reserves and at long last he was home. An interesting side note: Harry's good friend Eddy Frankiewicz decided that the regular Navy was alright with him and remained with the Navy rising to the rank of commander.

Harry liked the reserves. It was a place where he knew the rules, how to apply them and sometimes how to stretch them.

"I used to go over to Floyd Bennett Field, in New York City, in Brooklyn at the end of Flatbush Avenue and say, 'Hey, I would like to borrow a plane for the weekend.'

"'Oh, sure, what would you like?' They would say, 'We've got F6Fs, Corsairs, R4Ds, PBYs, we have JRBs, PBFs, what would you like?'

"'Let me have an R4D.'

"It was one of my all-time favorite airplanes and the all-time favorite airplane of most every pilot that flew them. I would use my wife Norine as the copilot and sit her in the right-hand seat and we would fly to Miami for the weekend. In those days nothing was organized, the war was over. We would stop at Opa Locka Naval Air Station down there and tell the guy to fill it up, we didn't even have to sign a chit or anything; there was no paperwork involved. We would spend the weekend there and come home Sunday night and then go to work the next morning.

"I guess it wasn't long after that, that was 1947, we started having to sign a chit to take the airplane and sign a chit to take fuel at the air stations. They finally got organized and organized squadrons and the squadrons were filled with reserve officers who were in active duty in a particular type of squadron. I was in a VR squadron, a transport squadron, so I was assigned to reserve transport squadron. The fighter pilots would be assigned to reserve fighter pilot squadrons, torpedo bomber pilots were assign to DB squadron. All during that time I flew quite a bit, mostly R4Ds and R5Ds.

"The DC-4 was the aircraft that was used most in moving reserve squadrons around the country. The reserve program called for weekend drills and two weeks of active duty, what they called 'ACDUTRA,' Active Duty for Training. The VR squadron spent two weeks in New Orleans, another squadron would be assigned to Oakland and so forth. I did an awful lot of that when I was a member of the VR reserve squadron; VR832 was the number of that squadron.

"Because our flights usually left Saturday morning, in order to go back on active duty for that weekend, we had to get a physical and sign out with the officer of the day. Well, he wouldn't be available early Saturday morning, so we would sign out, then I would run over at lunch time to LaGuardia, where I worked for the CAA, and I had the medical people sign my orders to say I was medically fit to check out the plane; it would take about an hour, go back to work at LaGuardia, then take off early the next morning for wherever.

"We would go out on Saturday and return on Sunday. We would get back too late to get checked out by the officer of the day and the medical people on Sunday, so I would have to run over during lunch time on Monday and go through the paperwork. As a result I would get paid for four days, only two days of flying but I would get paid for four days. Consequently, one year lets say, 1948, I made more money flying Navy reserves around the country than I did when I was an inspector for the CAA. There was hardly a weekend that went by I didn't do that, except the weekend I was assigned to Floyd Bennett Field."

"The weekends in the reserve program consisted of four drills: Saturday morning, Saturday evening, Sunday morning and Sunday evening. You needed a minimum of fifteen drills a year to get credit for a satisfactory year. Of course the retirement was based on the points you earned in reserve program so naturally I earned an awful lot of points doing all that flying for them.

"In the two-weeks active duty we would maybe fly down to Miami and be based in Miami or stay at Floyd Bennett Field as a transport squadron, then we would fly transport flights all over the country to different Naval air stations. We never went out of the country unless we had a set of orders signed by the chief of Naval Reserve training; they would sign the orders then we would go to places like Guantanamo Bay, Cuba, Trinidad, Coco Solo Naval Air Stations, that type thing. Otherwise the flights had to stay in the country.

"The reason why I mention that is because when a severe hurricane hit the gulf coast of Mexico, I was on weekend duty and was on my way to Guantanamo Bay, Cuba, which is on the east end of Cuba, and even though we had all those troubles with Castro, that Naval air station still belonged to the U.S.. I got in to Miami that Friday night and the next morning there was a set of orders for the operation: 'Proceed immediately to Scott Air Force Base, Bellevue, Illinois,' which was just across the river from St. Louis. It was an operation to supply the people of Tampico, Mexico, with emergency food and supplies and medical equipment and so on. Well, this one colonel said to me, 'We are going to use your R5D because it has two big cargo doors and we're going to have you fly a water purification system to Tampico.'

"I said, 'Well, I can't do that!'

"He said, 'Well, why not?'

"I said, 'This is a reserve airplane, I cannot leave the country without a set of orders from the chief of the reserve training.'

"'You don't fly for the Navy this weekend, son, you are flying for the Air Corps.'

"So they proceeded to load the biggest piece of machinery I have ever seen loaded on an airplane, a water purifier. They loaded it on the airplane and I flew it down to Corpus Christi, which was designated control point for this whole operation. I checked into operations and got instructions on what to do and

I told them I would need a flight kit. Well, they were all out of flight kits. I told them I needed at least a chart, and they said, 'We're all out of charts.'

"They said, 'Don't worry, we have got a carrier based right off the coast at Tampico and they have a non-directional beacon, you can home in on them.'

"I said that would be OK and asked, 'What is the frequency for that beacon?'

"'I don't know, we don't have any more information on that.'

"I said, 'You are sending me down to a strange country into an airport I have never been in and I don't have any charts, I don't have any frequencies and I don't know what I am going to do when I get there?'

"He said, 'Well, you better hurry up and do it because it is going to be dark by the time you get there!'

"So I took off and headed down to Tampico, landed just about dark with no lights on the runway. It turned out that Tampico did not have large enough forklifts to unload this massive piece of machinery out of my airplane.

"So I said, 'I have got to get that thing off, I can't fly that back to the States, get two forklifts.'

"So they brought in two of their biggest forklifts and slid them under this big piece of machinery and I told them to raise it up six inches and we threw a big line around the tail of that R5D, hooked it to a tractor and pulled the tail away from the load, and finally got it out onto the ground.

"I had a navigator on that trip that worked as a model in New York and he was an amateur photographer. He was meant to be movie cameraman, and director. He took aerial shots of the area around Tampico and all the flood damage and when we got back to New York that night, he sold them to one of the big TV stations and they were the first pictures to arrive in America from that Tampico flood."

"The reserve program was absolutely full of joy for me; I loved doing what I was doing. I loved flying people and cargo and mail everywhere. But one of the most interesting flights I

RESERVES

had was in October of 1955. I went out for my weekend and my mission that day was to fly to Stewart Air Force Base, which is directly across the river from West Point and pick up Henry Forrestal, the brother of James Forrestal, who was the Secretary of the Navy and the first Secretary of Defense. He jumped out of a window at Bethesda Naval Hospital.

"I was to pick up his older brother Henry and about forty or forty-five other Forrestal people and take them down to Norfolk for the commissioning of the carrier *Forrestal*.

"I'm in operations getting briefed for this flight, and I was introduced to this admiral, J. J. Clark. Everybody called him 'Jocko.' He was the leading admiral in the Pacific during the Korean War. He was to the Korean War what 'Bull' Halsey was to WW II in the Pacific. Jock was in his Mufti's, which means civvies, and he was going to ride with us down to the commissioning; he was retired and in New York at that time.

"He loved Naval aviators; he couldn't do enough for them. So he wanted to know if he could ride in the jump seat, which is the seat between the two pilot seats.

"I told him, 'Admiral, you are more than welcome.'

"I was a commander at the time and he said, 'You're a good kid, you're a good kid.'

"Saturday was a beautiful day for flying; beautiful day for anything; fishing, screwing or anything else you wanted to do. We circled Stuart AFB and there on the ramp, was the entire United States Military Academy of West Point student body of cadets, with all the VIPs standing in front of them standing at parade rest. So Jocko looks down there and after a few oaths, 'Goddamn, I don't want military honors, when we land go over and tell that goddamn general I don't want military honors!'

"'Yes, sir!'

"So I parked the airplane, climbed down the ladder, I'm in my aviation green uniform, which was a working uniform for the winter. I marched smartly up to this general, I think he was a two-star general as I recollect. Ribbons from hither to yon, I salute him smartly and he returns the salute smartly and in my best Naval language I say, 'Admiral Clark requests that you dispense with military honors, please sir!

"He looks at me and says, 'Admiral who?'

"'J. J. Clark.'

"'Never heard of him.'

"I said, 'Aren't these honors for him?'

"He said, 'Hell, no, these honors are for the secretary of the Army that is coming for the football game!'

"So I get back on the airplane, in the meantime they are loading the Forrestal clan on the airplane and I go up to the flight deck; he had to get up so I could get in.

"I said, 'It's all taken care of admiral, you don't even have to get off the airplane.'

"'Good boy, son, good boy!'

"Well, we get down to Norfolk and park on the VIP strip and the captain of the air station is there in his dress blues. When we taxied up on the VIP strip, there were about ten or twelve big black Cadillac limousines. At the end of that line was a gray Navy bus, like school bus but Navy gray. The captain said to the admiral, 'Admiral, you will be in the first limousine.'

"Clark said, 'Where are my pilots going to ride?'

"'Oh, they'll be in the bus.'

"Clark said, 'If they are in the bus, then that's where I'll be; in the bus!'

"So we went to the ship in a gray Navy bus when we could have had a big Navy limo. In the meantime Admiral Clark invited the copilot and myself to be his guests at the commissioning of the *Forrestal*.

"I said, 'We can't do that!' we're in our working uniforms, we can't go on board a commissioning service.

"First of all you have to have an invitation, second you have to be in uniform and the uniform of the day of a commissioning of a ship is dress blue bravo. That is white hat cover, gray gloves, hard metals and swords. He is dressed in Mufti's. He said, 'Don't worry about it.'

"I said, 'I've never been to a commissioning of a ship is there something I should know about the protocol and procedures?'

"'Well, sonny, just follow me and do what I do!'

RESERVES

"So we go on board and salute the fantail and follow him and the first thing the admiral says is, 'Charlie, how the hell are you, come on over, I want you to meet my pilots.'

"Charlie is Charles Thomas, Secretary of the Navy.

"'Hey Burke, come over here I want you to meet my pilots.'

"Arley Burke. Arley, '31-knot Burke' the famous destroyer commander in WW II, who was now chief of Naval operations in the Navy.

"Then he told someone, 'I want you to set two seats up in the gold section for my two pilots.'

"They said, 'Admiral, do you know what you are asking me?'

"'Do, it!'

"You were supposed to have a gold invitation card to get up there and there we were in our working uniforms because we are Admiral Clark's pilots!

"When it came time for the dedication speech, it was given by Burke, chief of Naval operations, he said, 'I'm not going to bore you with a long speech, I'm awfully glad you are all here, but I do have a few things I would like to get off of my mind.'

"With that, he reached into his uniform and pulled out a big thick speech and commenced to read it word for word in a drone without ever looking up from that paper. It was probably one of the most boring speeches I have ever heard in my life and it was done by the chief of Naval operations! But we all had a good time, we toured the ship and saw the latest in carriers and had a great time all thanks to Jocko Clark!"

"There is another wonderful story about an admiral. When the Korean War broke out, the reserve officers on active reserve squadrons got letters of notification saying that they would be recalled to active duty if they met the criteria. There were three factors in the criteria for recall which were that you had to be thirty-five years of age or younger, you had to be lieutenant commander or less in rank and you had to have two or fewer children in your family.

"Well I was thirty-two, I was a lieutenant and I had two children, so I met the criteria. Everybody else who got that letter at Floyd Bennett Field got ordered back to active duty, except me. So I grabbed a Navy airplane and flew down to the Pentagon to find out what the hell they were doing to me.

"I found the guy who was in charge, an admiral and he said, 'You're not recalled because you don't fit the criteria.'

"Instead of saying, 'Yes I do admiral.' I said, 'Thanks very much, it's nice to know you.'

"So I went on home, and when I got home that evening waiting in the mail were my recall orders. The left hand didn't know what the right hand was doing!

"In those days you spent the first thirty days of recall at your home base before you were assigned your full time assignment. In those thirty days you flew a lot of different missions a lot of different places with a lot of different airplanes.

"One of my missions was to fly another admiral. Every Navy flyer's hero was Admiral William F. Halsey, 'Bull' Halsey, the most successful strategist the Navy had in WW II. He had retired and was living in New York; he was a widower.

"My mission was to fly him to Boston, for the commissioning of the heavy cruiser *Quincy*. He showed up in dress blue and we could hardly find our way out to the airplane it was so foggy. The whole east coast was foggy.

"I said, 'Well, the weather looks pretty bad but we'll give it a try.'

"So we took off and the closest airport that was open was Washington National Airport. That was our alternate for Boston if you can believe that! We headed up to Boston and did two ILS approaches and didn't even see the ground, the minimums were 200 feet and half a mile, and I cheated at least 100 feet on that second approach! I could never see the approach lights. So I climbed up and called the approach control and told them I would like a radar vector over to Squantum, Massachusetts, and try to shoot a GCA approach over there if that was OK with them. They said, 'Hell, you can do anything you want, you are the only airplane flying in New England today!'

"So they vectored me over to Squantum Naval Air Station and I couldn't get onto GCA. GCA minimums are 100 feet and a quarter of a mile but I couldn't pick up the lights on the runway.

"I climbed back up and went back to talk to Admiral Halsey. The DC-3 had twenty-five seats on it and he was the only one on board. He was sitting there reading the *New York Herald Tribune*, which was still being published back in those days and drinking out of a thermos jug.

"So I told him that it didn't look good for us to get into Boston but I'm going to give it one more try and I am going to try to get in to Quonset Point Naval Air Station on Narragansett Bay and if I could get him in there, there would still be time to get him to the Boston Navy Yard. He said to me, 'Well, don't sweat it, I don't want to give this frappin' speech anyhow so don't sweat it.'

"We couldn't get in at Quonset Point and by this time we had been in the air about three hours and I was pouring sweat. I finally went back and told the admiral we were returning to New York and he said, 'Good!'

"So I landed and I had to make three GCA approaches before I could land it at Floyd Bennett Field, that's how low that weather was. We taxied up to the VIP strip and there was the captain of the air station and the executive officer with a big black limo. He was looking at me with daggers; if looks could kill I would have been dead on the spot! He said, 'What the hell did you bring him back here for?!'

"So Halsey got off and they put him in the back seat of the limousine and he next thing I know the executive officer comes up, 'Admiral Halsey wants to see you.' I was covered with sweat after flying three or four hours in the worst weather and fog, I'm stripped down to my skivvies shirt so I had to get my shirt on, put on my tie, put on my green blouse, put on my hat and go out and see the admiral, which I do. He was sitting in the rear seat of the limousine with the door open, and the captain of the air station is sitting in the other side of him.

"He said, 'Son, I just want to tell you that is one of the greatest jobs of flying I have ever seen.'

"He shakes my hand, and this is Admiral Halsey! It was the highest compliment he could have paid me.

"With that the captain smiled and looked like, 'Ah, yes one of my boys, terrific Bernard, terrific!'

"So I said, 'Well, Admiral, we can get you there 99 and 44/100 percent of the time but in flying you can't beat the weather, there is no way you can beat the weather.'

"'Well,' he said, 'If you remember your fucking history in WW II, I sank half the fucking 3rd fleet trying to get through a fucking typhoon going into Okinawa against the goddamn fucking advice of all my senior staff officers; you don't have to tell me about the weather!'

"But that was the kind of guy he was, damn the torpedoes, full speed ahead! He was man of action. But I'm sure he regretted the loss of life in that operation."

"When I got recalled to active duty, I was assigned to the commander of the Atlantic fleet, headquartered in Norfolk, Virginia. The personnel officer was a buddy of mine from WW II and he said to me, 'Bernard, what the hell are you doing here, you are not a VP pilot you're a VR pilot!'

"I said, 'Well, these are my orders Pete.'

"He said, 'I don't understand this at all, you know what I have to do with you?'

"'No, what do you have to do with me?'

"'I have to assign you to FAETULANT, Fleet Airborne Electronics Training Unit, Atlantic fleet to train you on anti-submarine warfare.'

"I said, 'Well, that doesn't sound like very good duty to me, I'll be in school every day, all damn day long and night for six weeks!'

"He said, 'Go check into FAETULANT then check into BOQ and come back.'

"So I checked into FAETULANT and one of the yeomen said to me, 'Commander Brown wants to see you.'

"I said, 'No, I just left his office a few minutes ago.'

"'Well, he just called a minute ago and wants to see you right away.'

"I went back to see Pete and he's got another officer in his office, I believe it was a Commander Lawrence. So Peter introduced me to Commander Lawrence and we made some small talk and one thing or another and I wondered who the hell this Commander Lawrence was. Finally he gets around to telling me that Commander Lawrence is my new executive officer VP11 operating under Comfair 3 headquartered in Argentia, Newfoundland.

"Argentia, Newfoundland, would be a candidate for the world's worst weather. There is always fog coming in off the Grand Banks.

"I said, 'Well, I thought you were going to send me to FAETULANT?'

"He said, 'Let me worry about that, I want a pilot that can fly all weather in that damn fog we've got in Newfoundland, I'll put a PP1P, that's a copilot, that can use all the equipment you just fly the airplane and get us in and out of there! You leave in a half an hour.'

"So I got back, I actually hadn't unpacked, but I load my gear on a PB4Y2, that is exactly the same as the B-24 Liberator, except it only had a single tail. It was an antisubmarine warfare plane loaded with equipment. So we go on up to Argentia, and the next day I meet the skipper and then the operations officer designated me a patrol plane commander. It was the first time I'd ever seen the airplane. I had never been checked out in the airplane or anything and I am the damn pilot in command of that airplane as an all-weather pilot.

"One day the skipper, Donald Wiss, called me in and says, 'We're getting P2V5Fs, we're getting rid of these buckets of bolts, I want you to go back to Quonset Point, Rhode Island, and get checked out in a P2V5F.'

"I said, 'What school do they have in Quonset Point, Rhode Island?'

"He says, 'They don't have a school down there, our sister squadron VP8 will check you out.'

"Well, he didn't make any arrangements or anything, he just left it to my ingenuity to go down and get checked out in the most complex airplane the Navy had, the P2V5F. A patrol plane, it had eleven crew members on it, a PPC, PP1P, the plane captain, which we called the flight engineer in the Navy, navigator, two sonar operators, two radar operators, two electronic countermeasures operators, and two MAD [Magnetic Anomaly Detection] operators. When a submarine goes through the water it disturbs the lines of magnetic variation and that can be picked up with the MAD system. It is so accurate, it is the final system used to trap the submarine. That involves maneuvers at a maximum height of 300 feet. When you do that at night, out over the middle of the Atlantic Ocean, your copilot has his eyes riveted to that radar altimeter ready to tap you on the shoulder and help you pick your nose up!

"I checked in with the skipper of VP8, I knew him. He said, 'What are you doing down here, you are supposed to be in Newfoundland?'

"I said, 'Yeah, I'm down here so you can check me out in the P2V.'

"He says, 'You've got to be kidding!'

"'No, Don Wiss sent me down here to get checked out in the P2V, I'm serious!'

"He says, 'There is no way I can check you out in the P2V, we just got back from deployment in Iceland, we've got 100 percent turnover in my PPCs, I've got to upgrade all my PP1Ps to left seat PPCs. I've got all the training and we still have that 600-hour commitment to the fleet for ASW. I don't have the fuel, I don't have the people, I don't have the inclination to check you out in the P2V!'

"I said, 'You couldn't expect me to go back to Newfoundland and tell the skipper I failed my mission!'

"'Well, I don't know what else you are going to do, I don't know how you are going to say that you failed your mission!'

"I said, 'Look, for old time sake, how about checking me out, I'm a quick learner.'

"He relented and finally said, 'OK I'll tell you what I will do. I will give you a flight check, one ride. If you can hack the mustard, I'll sign you off, if you can't, you can go back to Newfoundland with your head bowed.'

RESERVES

"I said, 'OK, give me a few days, I'll read the manuals and handbooks and everything else, sit in the cockpit and get a good cockpit check and get familiar with it.'

"He said, 'Get your flight suit on, we are going right now!'

"I got my flight suit on and off we go to this P2V5F.

"The P2V5F was a long-range patrol bomber. It had two Curtiss-Wright turbo compound engines, which means that of the twelve cylinders in the radial engines, four cylinders' exhaust gasses were collected in a turbine and was shafted in the main crank shaft and gave it another 100 horsepower or so. We had three power recovery turbines on those engines so we got another 300 horsepower from the exhaust gasses. It was a very complex engine. It was also an automatic feathering engine. It had these great big paddle blades that would be like barn doors, and would cause a lot of drag if you didn't handle them right.

"So I start the engines, and he started telling me the auto power settings, I said, 'Yeah, I'm familiar with that, that's the same setting we use on a Convair 240.'

"He finished telling me about speeds and I said, 'Those are the same speeds as on the Convair 240.'

"The whole thing flew like a Convair 240. So we taxied out to the jet runway, runway 16, and took off. We got about 100 feet in the air, the landing gear hadn't sucked in to the engine nacelles yet, when the right engine explodes and feathers. I started to bank the airplane and he says, 'Straighten the airplane up!'

"'I said, 'Why?'

"He said, 'Let's try to get a little altitude and we'll figure out what the hell to do!'

"I said, 'I know what the hell I'm going to do, I'm going to land it on that other runway right there!'

"I took off on the long runway 16, and I had to make steep turn to get it in there, but I was under control all the way. I made the turn to the crosswind runway, number 28, and I used about half of the short runway, did a single engine reverse to stop it and he said, 'Keerist, if you can do that, give me your log book, I'll sign it!'

"I was still at Quonset Point, Rhode Island, when I got an aircraft transport order. The first airplane was to be picked up at Jacksonville, the modification center. So I hitched a ride down in a Navy airplane, and the signing commander, which is the modification center executive, allows each acceptance flight test pilot thirty minutes of fuel, the Navy was very particular about 'bravo funds,' which was the fuel costs. Hell, thirty minutes wasn't enough for me to get thoroughly familiar with this airplane. I had never stalled one; I didn't know what its flight characteristics were. So I was gone for six hours. I went over to Cecil Field and I was shooting touch-and-goes, I was doing stalls, steep turns, just learning my airplane. When I came back down after six hours, you would have thought that I had just killed the commanding officer of the Naval air station. They were so upset that I had used six hours of fuel instead of thirty minutes of fuel. But we straightened it out.

"We were a twelve-plane squadron, all of them P2V5Fs with those Curtiss-Wright 3350 PRT engines, plus two jet engines on pods under the wings, two J34 jet engines. We used to say, 'two to turn and two to burn.' I took the first one back to Quonset Point, went back and got the second one, went back got the third one and went back and got the fourth one. I picked up all twelve airplanes at Jacksonville and ferried them up to Quonset Point. That gave me about fifty hours in that airplane and by the time I had delivered the twelfth airplane I was beginning to feel like I was familiar although every airplane was different. The landing light switches were in one place in one airplane and in another place in another plane. That was the way they came out of the standardization center; very unstandardized.

"But by the end of the twelfth airplane I felt very good about that airplane. It was a very good airplane to fly but it had one bad feature. In order to keep the MAD antenna away from all the electronic systems in the airplane they built a big fiberglass stinger tail, and the antenna was at the end of that, but that gave it a bad crosswind-handling characteristic. So you had to have good crosswind-landing technique, which was not too hard to do but some of the guys never did get it. The airplane had such a bad reputation, I should say the pilots were so afraid of it that Lockheed sent a demonstration pilot out to visit all the VP squadrons that had P2Vs to demonstrate the good parts of this airplane.

"Aerodynamically, it was a wonderful airplane, but it had its bad parts. Besides the crosswind problems, it grossed at 80,000 pounds, max gross weight, and the handbook said it is estimated that the aircraft will be able to sustain level flight at 62,000 pounds gross weight. That's 18,000 pounds below the gross weight of the airplane, which meant every time you took off you were 18,000 pounds over gross!

"We carried 8,000 pounds of bombay stores; special weapons that we could release. In addition we had wing tip pods. The starboard wing tip had a 350-gallon tank and it had a seventy-million candle power controllable light. The copilot had a handgrip and he could control the light in elevation and azimuth for picking up surfaced submarines at night. The carbon filament was thicker than your thumb, and you could only operate it two minutes out of five. Two minutes on then three minutes to cool before you could use it again. That 350-gallon tank was about 2,100 pounds plus the weight of the light. The port tip tank had the 350-gallon tank and a NAPS-42 antenna for radar. So that's another 2,100 pounds of fuel plus the weight of the antenna and the machinery for operating the antenna.

"So we could dump about 5,000 pounds of weight just by hitting one pickle [ejection] button. Each of those tip tanks had a 3,000-pound concussion spring in it. When you pushed that ejection button for those tip tanks and the bombay, that 3,000-pound spring threw that weight out both sides.

"The airplane would not stall. You could climb that airplane, and these maneuvers I learned from the demonstration pilot from Lockheed, you could put that airplane in a steep climb with METO power, which was maximum except takeoff. You could keep steepening the climb until the airplane went into a stall buffet so violent that you could hardly hang onto the wheel! With all this buffeting, there was no tendency for a wing to droop; the airplane would climb 500 or 600 feet a minute. It was very unusual.

"Another method we used for instilling confidence in our pilots was we would simulate a circling approach to an airport, and put the airplane into a forty-five-degree bank and we would keep tightening the turn. The angle of bank won't change but you would tighten the turn until you get a stall buffet. When that happened, you reached up and pulled the bottom engine. Pulling it into a deep buffet stall, we rolled it out of that into a right bank, still in a deep buffet stall and never lose a foot of altitude! That is a performing airplane! I don't believe there is another airplane that can do that. Needless to say it was one of my favorite airplanes of all times."

"When I was released from active duty when the Korean War was over I went back to my CAA job and my old reserve squadron at Floyd Bennet Field, VR32. In the late 50s, I'm not sure of the year, the CAA needed a helicopter-qualified pilot that could perform flight checks and line checks to New York Airways, which was a helicopter airline. It was one of three in the U.S.. One was in Los Angeles, one was in Chicago and one was in New York. They asked me if I would take the job if I got qualified and I said, 'sure.'

"I was always glad to get qualified in new equipment. So we bought twenty-five hours of instruction from the chief pilot, Les Carter, of New York Airlines. I learned to fly in an H-19, military designation was the S-55, which carried eight passengers in the cabin. The engine was in the front; it had a Curtiss-Wright R1820 engine. The two pilots sat above the engine and the shaft went right through the cockpit into the gearbox that drove the rotors. I did quite a few flight checks and type ratings in that during the next few years. And in 1957, the administrator of the CAA was James Pyle, was at a cocktail party and he ran into a good friend of his named Garrison Norton who was secretary of the Navy for air. Garrison said to Jimmy, 'What the hell do we have to do to fly a Navy helicopter through your air traffic control system?'

"Jimmy says, 'Hell if I know, give me a helicopter and we'll check it out.'

RESERVES

"So the Navy bought a brand new S-58 helicopter right off the line, the military designation is the H-34. And they gave it to us for twelve months to develop procedures for certifying pilots for helicopter flying. The Navy said they would equip the helicopter and maintain it.

"Well, I picked it up at Sikorsky and flew it down to Patuxent River, and turned it over to electronics test. And we gave them one of each navigation radio that we used in the system for them to install in the helicopter. They gave us a thirty-day estimate and it took them ninety days to equip it, mainly because they couldn't find a place to put the glide slope antenna because of what they called rotor modulation. They finally got it done and now we only had nine months to do the program.

"In those nine months I only flew when the weather was very bad. Even in fact when some airports were closed. We flew most of the time out of the Marine base at Quantico, Virginia, and all our service was done by service techs at Patuxent River. For nine months we flew it 375 hours, all on heavy instruments.

"We never had any problems except for one time. I used as copilots several helicopter-qualified inspectors. Well, I had a fellow by the name of 'Hap' Law, Howard G. Law. He was an air carrier inspector from LaGuardia. We got into a heavy thunderstorm and I had always maintained that if I had to be in a heavy thunderstorm, I would rather be in a helicopter than a fixed wing airplane. But I changed my mind when I got into this one! It was a severe level-five or six thunderstorm, and it pitched my nose up so violently that I got blade stall and had the cyclic pitch all the way forward and the nose still pitched up and over I went on my back and tumbled out of the bottom of that thunderstorm. I was over the Kenton VOR, which was on the Delaware River, and I proceeded to Dover Air Force Base as soon as possible so I could change my underwear! I was punching little holes in that leather seat with my butt!

"It scared the hell out of me! Being upside down in a thunderstorm in a helicopter, I was in one in an airplane one time but this was a lot more severe.

"I remember taking off from Washington National one time on a high wind situation and we climbed those things at sixty knots. The controller asked for my position and I gave it to him and he said, 'Well, I don't know, I've got a stationary target at 6,000 feet over there, is that you?'

"I said, 'That's me!'"

Based in part on Harry's recommendations, it was concluded that helicopters could indeed be flown purely on instruments. This led the way for the helicopter being used in many more forms including the Coast Guard whose missions often occur during bad weather or storms.

That wasn't the extent of Harry's helicopter experience as I was soon to find out when I noticed an interesting picture in Harry's bedroom.

5
WHIRLYBIRDS

On one of my trips to see Harry for an interview, I asked about all of the artifacts collected in the lower rooms of his condominium. There were large-scale maps, pictures of friends, a picture of the Air Force precision flying team, the Thunderbirds, personally inscribed to Harry. There was an old Sensenich propeller above the doorway, and letters of congratulations and commendation scattered on the walls. But over his bed something caught my eye. A black and white picture that I knew I had seen before. There was an inscription on the lower right corner and I walked nearer to read it. As I drew closer, Harry saw my interest and began to speak.

"That is Sikorsky flying the VS-300 helicopter; the first successful helicopter. That was tethered because it was the first flight and he taught himself to fly it because it was a lot easier to fly it himself than it was to teach someone else to fly the helicopter. This shows Sikorsky in a black overcoat and his trademark black fedora. I was in Igor's office with one of his right-hand people named Ted Dumont. Also in that meeting was Ralph Lightfoot who was the chief engineer for Sikorsky

WHIRLYBIRDS

and 'Jimmy' Viner, Dimitri was his first name; he was Sikorsky's nephew.

"So after the meeting was over I said to Igor, 'Igor, I look at that picture and it brings back wonderful memories.'

"He said, 'How so Harry?' He spoke with a very heavy brogue.

"I said, 'Well, when I was in college I taught part-time at the Bridgeport Flying Service where that picture was taken, my future wife, Norine, came down to the airport and we were both there when you made that historic flight. We both got a thrill out of it and I think we both subconsciously knew what a major and significant feat that was.'

"He said, 'Oh, that's wonderful Harry!'

"Two weeks later in the mail came a framed picture identical to the one on his wall, which was inscribed, 'To Norine and Harry Bernard, with best wishes from Igor Sikorsky.'"

This was interesting to me because I knew that Harry flew airplanes with the greatest of ease, but I wondered what he was doing in the office of Igor Sikorsky. I asked Harry to expand on his helicopter experience and I got more than an earful. This was all new to me so we went back upstairs and put on the kettle for some more tea.

He began with a story about a heliport that New York Airways wanted to build on the Hudson River and then told a few stories of certifying different helicopters and a check ride that nearly cost him his life.

"One of the stickiest problems I had to work with in the helicopter phase of my career involved the Port of New York Authority, New York Airways and the CAA. The problem arose when we flight-checked the West 30th Street heliport; this was the first heliport in New York City, right on the Hudson River. After analysis and study we concluded that the best heliport location would be on the roof of the big pier building. Whereas the New York Authority wanted the heliport to be parallel to the river banks on a flat pier. Well, we hassled and fought about it and we wrote our report and recommendations and it became such a hassle that George Moore, the administrator came up from Washington and fought with them. All the port authority people were there who were involved with this including Austin J. Tobin who was the head of the Port of New York Authority.

"Well, we briefed the administrator, his name was Charles Lowe, on what we thought was the best orientation of the heliport on the top of the pier. Austin J. Tobin rose so much hell that the administrator backed off and said they would put it where Tobin wanted it. It turned out that we were fighting over more than just a heliport. The Port of New York Authority controlled the entire waterfront in New Jersey, they controlled the entire waterfront in Brooklyn but they didn't control any waterfront on the island of Manhattan. This was to get their foot in the door to get control of the waterfront in the city of Manhattan. Of course, we found that out later, they could care less where the heliport was, they needed that pier that was parallel to the river, that gave them control of that first piece of real estate on the Manhattan waterfront. It was a result of that 30th Street fiasco that they took me down to Washington; they thought I did a hell of a good job with that project.

"It wasn't long after I was down in Washington, of course I had to learn all the headquarters policies, one of which was that no CAA employee testified before congressional committee without the approval of the big wheels in the CAA and only to read from a written statement that was approved by the lawyers.

"Well, one of the CAA directors asked me to sit in on a congressional hearing at ten one morning. I got there early and one of the secretaries in the conference room said, 'You have plenty of time to go down and get a cup of coffee.'

"I said, 'What is this meeting about?'

"She said, 'I really can't tell you, I don't know.'

"So I went down and had a cup of coffee in the congressional dining room and I came back about five minutes to ten everybody was filing into the big hearing room. The secretary said, 'The director called, he wants you to call him.'

"So I called the number and got his secretary. She said, 'The director will not be able to testify today, he wants you to testify.'

"I said, 'What do you mean he wants me to testify, I can't testify, it's against agency policy for me to testify! What is the meeting about, I don't even know what the subject matter is!' I said.

"She said, 'Well, he didn't tell me but he said you would do a god job.'

"So in I go. Well, my first clue that it was about helicopters was when I saw Joe Mashman who was head of flight tests for Bell helicopters. I had worked with Joe on many committees. I saw him in the spectator's part of this hearing room. I couldn't talk to him, but I thought, hell, this must be about helicopters!

"The first witness is the director of flight operations and airworthiness bureau of the Civil Aeronautics Administration. Somebody said, 'I understand he will not testify, in his place will be Harry Bernard from the operations division of the CAA.'

"Normally when you testify before a congressional committee you are testifying as a technical expert. So you give them five minutes of who you are and where you are coming from and what qualifies you to be a technical expert in this hearing. Well, I did five or six minutes of that and the senator, who was from Maryland, he had had a stroke and he dangled a cigarette from the corner of his mouth and he was a mumbler as a result of the stroke. He asked me a question and I didn't hear a word he said, neither did the stenotypist. She said, 'Senator, would you mind repeating that question please?' And he said much more clearly this time, 'Well, are you appearing for or against this downtown heliport!'

"Oh, man the light bulb rang and I thought, oh, that's what I'm here about!

"'Yes, I am for the downtown heliport and against sin!'

"I gave about ten or fifteen minutes of what the standards were, where it should be located, what the protection for the public should be and a little technical talk.

"When I went back to the office that afternoon after lunch, I got a hold of my immediate boss, George Moore, and I said, 'George, you won't believe what happened to me today!'

"He said, 'What happened?'

"I said, 'I just testified ad-lib before a congressional committee!' and commenced to tell him the whole story.

"They could have hung me out to dry, I had violated every policy of the administrator by representing the agency in a congressional meeting.

"He said, 'Oh my God, you better write a memorandum telling me what happened for the record.'

"So I sat down and dictated a letter like he wanted. Unbeknownst to George, or me or a lot of people, the director, although he was top man in the agency, he was hen-pecked at home, he never liked to go home. He would come around at five o'clock when I was going home and say, 'Harry, I want to talk about something, stay tonight and we'll work it out.'

"We would go down to his office and we would work until nine, then we would go down and get a cracker and Coke and then at about eleven he would go on home. No one knew it, but he wandered around in the dark in the offices, looking at all the correspondence in the office that day to make sure nobody was trying to get him. Well, he ran across this memo I had written.

"The next morning I got called down to George Moore's office and he said, 'The director is demoting you one grade and sending you back to New York.'

"Well, the sending me back to New York was all right but not the demotion of one grade. So I said, 'If that's the way this agency works I am out of here, I quit!'

"I wrote my letter of resignation right there, I dictated to the girl, signed it and went home. Well, it got up to Jimmy Pyle, the administrator who had flown with me on this helicopter instrument program and the director got overruled at every angle and he almost lost his job over it. So I got to stay and I guess things worked out OK for me."

"When I was working with New York Airways, I had done some flight tests on a helicopter called the Vertol 107 built by Boeing Vertol, in Morton, Pennsylvania. The company was originally Piaseki helicopter. Then it became Vertol, then Boeing Vertol. It was a twin turbine helicopter and it went into service about the same time the Sikorsky S-61 went into service with the military and with Los Angeles Airways. At that time we were just beginning to think about operating from elevated buildings. I had attended a meeting in New York where the Wright brothers' memorial lecture was given at the Wings Club every year by a prominent notable aviation figure. That particular year it was given by Grover Loening, who was the first man to get an aeronautical engineering degree from any American college; from Columbia University. He was an early pioneer in the 20s and 30s. He built amphibious airplanes that he called the Loening air yacht. He gave the lecture and to make a long story short his thing was helicopters are the air transport of the future. That you would hit the elevator up button on a New York skyscraper go to the top floor where there would be a helipad, load in the helicopter, the helicopter would rise vertically and then the rotors would tilt forward and it would fly you at high speed to Honolulu. That was his dream; it was a very interesting talk. Of course we haven't reached that point but we do have a tilt wing rotor system now in the military the V-22 Osprey."

"At Sikorsky we had developed what we called a vertical takeoff technique. In which from an extremely elevated platform you would takeoff backwards keeping that platform in front of you at all times until you reached a critical decision height, CDH, which was usually 110 feet depending on the weight and temperature and other things. It was similar to the V1-V2 concept of a horizontal take off of an airplane on a runway. If the engine quits before V1 you stop, if the engine quits after V1 you keep going to V2 and climb out. This is the same concept, if the engine quit before you reached the critical decision height you would descend on the other engine back to the platform. If you didn't lose an engine you would go into transitional flight and climb on out.
"So New York gets the Vertol 107 twin turbine tandem rotor helicopter. It carried I think twenty-four passengers. The eastern region where I had previously worked insisted that if New York Airways was to be approved from the top of the Pan American skyscraper in mid-Manhattan they would have to

demonstrate flight from that elevated platform before the region would approve it. Well, New York Airways refused. They insisted on doing all their flight check work from the top of their transportation building at the site of the old New York World's Fair, which I think was around five stories. It was built in the form of a 'T' so you really had two runways as it were. The eastern region would not approve that operation without actual flight and cutting engines from the top of the Pan Am building. So New York Airways appealed to Washington headquarters and the project was put in the hands of a fellow named Ward Madsen, one of my bosses. We developed what we called a multiple pilot evaluation team. In other words we would get a lot of qualified helicopter people and would look at it. Well, I was picked to represent the agency on that team and we went to Fort Belvior, their army helicopter contingent down there. The Marine Corps sent a colonel and major from Quantico, Virginia. The colonel was the commanding officer of an experimental VX squadron, which actually was the squadron that flew the president of the United States. We ended up having about ten highly qualified pilots on that team.

"At the first meeting, the Marine colonel said, 'There is no way I would fly the president off the top of the Pan Am building, no way!' He said it wasn't safe. That was also the consensus of most of the rest of the pilots on that team. In the meantime we had told New York Airways if it was problematic we were going to prove it by flying from the top of the Pan Am building. New York Airways met with Pan Am they said, 'We will pay for the insurance.' There was a very high premium for this test operation. So it came time to make the first flight.

"The first flight was flown by myself and Les Carter who had been my instructor and checked me out in the helicopter the year before. He was chief pilot of New York Airways. He wasn't too familiar with the vertical takeoff technique but they all became very familiar with it as time went on. We got on the top of the Pan Am building and he asked me if I would fly the first takeoff. I said, 'Well Les, you are the chief pilot of the company don't you want to?'

"He said, 'No, I'd rather you did this.'

"'Well, OK.'

"I think our critical decision height was 100 feet from the top of the building. So I said to Les, 'The first maneuver we are going to do is have an engine failure before we get to 100 feet so when I call for it, cut one engine.'

"He says, 'Are you sure?'

"I said, 'We are going to die in a blaze of glory here!'

"Well, at 100 feet I called 'cut' and he pulled one engine back but the other engine also came off line!"

Oh my....

"So I'm up there 100 feet over the Pan Am building hovering without any power. But all I did was put it in autorotation and land it right back on the platform; it was a piece of cake.

"We sat there, I looked at him and he looked at me and he said, 'Shit, is that all there is to that?'

"I said, 'That's it Les, that's it!'

"So I did a couple more with one engine helping us get back down instead of autorotating down. Then he did several and he said, 'Hell, that's no problem at all.'

"So about half the others had a try at it and we worked very late into the evening to come up with a consensus on the safety of the operation. Well, Ward, who headed up the team, he was not a helicopter man himself, but he was a very good administrator. He went around the room and I said, 'No sweat.' Les Carter said, 'No problem.'

"Some of the other assistant chief pilots said, 'No problem.' In the meantime the Marine major fell asleep in this meeting. When it came around to the colonel he said, 'Well, I came in here convinced it couldn't be safe, but after watching it and after flying it, no sweat.'

"Apparently he hadn't discussed his position with the major. Ward said, 'Major, what do you think?'

"He woke up and said, 'I agree with the colonel, we can't do this there is no safety involved!'

"There was of course a loud chuckle around the room!

"But we approved it and it was a very successful operation carrying thousands of passengers from the Pan Am building in mid-Manhattan to Newark Airport, LaGuardia, Kennedy. Until one day, a helicopter was loading passengers, there were a dozen and a half passengers waiting to get on, and they were standing up on the roof in the passenger waiting area. One of the helicopter's main gears collapsed and the helicopter tilted over, and the shrapnel killed four people waiting to get on the flight. It was a terrible tragedy. It was a mechanical failure, one shot in a million but it was the end of helicopter operations. The public outcry was so loud that New York Airways closed and so did the other two carriers.

"People in New York were very hard to convince that the helicopter was safe. For example: During the period of time when they only flew mail, they wanted to start operations in Fairlawn, New Jersey. It was the center of the industrial complex; a lot of mail and packages were generated. It developed into a public hearing over the safety of this heliport. They asked me if I would appear and give a pitch about safety, which I did. Everything was going fine until this one native of Fairlawn, who was a local hero up there, stood up in his WW II Army Air Corps uniform and said, 'As you all know, I flew B-24s in WW II and I was shot down and I'm here to tell you aviation is not safe!' They turned the heliport down on the basis of that speech by the WW II guy."

Sometimes, even in the face of overwhelming support, emotions win out and illogical decisions are made on the basis of fraud. How might aviation travel be different today if such pursuit of helicopter travel was maintained? Perhaps we would be hopping on helicopters for short jaunts instead of hopping on the bus. A helicopter pad can be built nearly anywhere as evidenced by the presence of helipads on nearly every trauma hospital in the United States. An intriguing thought, one that Harry thinks has too often been overlooked. But coming from a man with such passion for the air it is natural to think that he would want to expand aviation to all possible venues.

> *The next few stories are ones that were remembered by my prodding, having seen unusual comments in the margins of Harry's rather extensive logbooks. Each should be taken on its own, they are not in any sort of chronological order; they are simply small pieces of smoldering tinder that I made glow for a while.*

"Before I went to Washington, the CAA had no helicopters of its own, so we purchased time from helicopter operators. One of them was New England Airways; they were based up in Providence, Rhode Island. We would buy five hours of flight time for each CAA man who was helicopter qualified. We got our helicopter training and our proficiency practice flying out at Zohn's airfield on Long Island, and our instructor was a Frenchman by the name of Maurice Paquette. I had never flown a small helicopter before and it was my turn to go fly this Bell-47. Everything I had flown until then was the S-55s up through the biggies. So he says, 'You've never flown a Bell helicopter, how did you learn to fly?'

"I said, 'My first helicopter was a Sikorsky S-55.'

"'Wow, big!' he says.

"It was a very windy day, this is very vivid in my mind, we flew twenty minutes and Maurice says, 'Put it down, you are fine to fly by yourself, do what you want.'

"But I had to get ballast. When you fly the helicopter from the right, when there is another person in the left seat, it is OK, but when you fly it solo, the helicopter has to carry weight on the left side to compensate for the lost rider. So I kept the rotor turning and he went to the back of his car to get ballast. He came back he said, 'I can't find it, but don't worry, you can fly good.'

"I said, 'Yeah, but don't you need ballast?'

"He said, 'Yeah but you fly good.'

"So I pulled the collective up and put the helicopter into a hover. About that time a gust of wind hit the helicopter and I had full rudder and the helicopter tail swung around in the wind, but she came back. So I am getting ready to take off when two dogs come running out from somewhere on the airport, get underneath that helicopter jumping up and barking at me, so I

I checked in the BOQ and the fellow who had the room next to me was in charge of the ground school training. He said, 'I'll tell you what, if you buy the beer, I'll do the tutoring in the evening.'

"So that's how it went. He tutored me to the point where, I didn't ace the exams, but I did very well on all the exams and passed all of them. The next morning, McDaniel took me out and I did flight A-1 and A-15, the flight checks for the phase. That was in the morning. In the afternoon after lunch, I flew B-1 and B-15, so I got through the first thirty hours of the syllabus. The next morning we started the C phase and both it and the D phase were done in the HUP-2, a tandem-rotor helicopter. The helicopter had servos to relieve the pilot of the pressure but you had to do all the flight training with the servos off, I mean you had to manhandle that machine; it was hard work.

"By this time, McDaniel had assigned a new instructor because he was too busy doing other things. About four hours in this HUP-2 I said, 'I quit, I can't handle this damn helicopter with the servos off, I don't have the strength!'

"He said, 'Look, everybody quits right away, another couple of hours and it will come to you, I guarantee it!'

"And sure enough he was right, after a couple more hours, and a lot of it was autorotations, I got used to it. So I completed the C phase. Then he says, 'You can skip whatever part of the D phase you want, we can take the D phase flight check.'

"Well, I took most of it because a lot of it was load lifting, sky crane operations and getting carrier qualified. Landing aboard a carrier is a piece of work! The wind direction and velocity are extremely important in helicopters. The wind streaks on the water are going one way, the smoke coming out of the stacks is going another way, the relative wind flag held by a sailor is going another. But you always go on that relative flag; once you get a hang of that it becomes easy. I think it was twenty landings on a carrier to get qualified. Then I did short-field landings, remote area work and a lot of operations problems.

"I completed the D check and I think I still had two days to go of these fourteen days. The skipper wanted to see me and I went down to see him and he said, 'Well, I'll be dipped in shit, I

WHIRLYBIRDS

didn't think it could be done!' So I got my helicopter rating and I got my diploma."

Harry then became skipper of HS832 at Floyd Bennett Field in New York. Mainly they were a submarine hunting unit. Flying a big Sikorsky S-58, they would hover about 100 feet over the water and drop a big ball antenna into the water to send out pings and receive echoes back to help determine the location of submarines.

Later in 1956, Harry had what I think is the closest call of them all. He had returned to giving flight checks for helicopters and late one evening, Harry was approached to do a rush job on a type rating. Harry's instincts were spot on ... he shouldn't have done it. But pressure from his superiors said otherwise. It is often said haste makes waste, but in this case it cost a life, nearly two.

"It was Friday at 5:00, and we were just getting ready to scurry off, when New York Airways called. They said they had just hired a pilot out of the Marine Corps and they needed to get him a type rating flight check in a helicopter so he could fly his schedule the next day. I said, 'No, I don't do flight checks at night in a helicopter.'

"Well, it wasn't long after that the president of New York Airways, Jack Gallagher, called me. 'We need him!'

"I said, 'Jack, we can't give flight checks at night, we do some pretty hairy stuff!'

"'Well, Harry we have got to have him in the morning for schedule.'

"'No way Jack.'

"About five minutes later, my boss called and said, 'Do it!'

"So I said, OK and went over to New York Airways. The pilot's name was Lunn, Jim Lunn. We introduced ourselves and chatted for a few minutes and I said, 'Let's go.'

"Well, he was very nervous, but he did a very good job. We went through all the maneuvers for the type rating flight check. The most critical maneuver we did on the flight check was an autorotation where we were at 500 feet and we did a 360 turn on the way down to land. Autorotation turns the helicopter into an autogyro so instead of the engine driving the rotor, your speed through the air drives the rotor, because you are disconnected from the gearbox. It's like when you were a kid and you stuck the windmill out the window of the car and watched it spin. So it's a bang-bang maneuver.

"We did this whole flight check at one of the unused runways at LaGuardia, runway 23. Well, when we came out of that maneuver, he was a little bit late; we hit very hard. But I had hit a lot harder than that in that helicopter many times, and I had hit hard when I was flying it myself. This helicopter, although it was a brand new helicopter, apparently had a fracture in the left landing gear strut. The left landing gear strut had a crash stop, which prevented it, in case of a hard landing, from going into the main fuel tank. Well, the crash stop didn't stop the strut. There must have been a crack or something somewhere. The left gear collapsed and went into the fuel tank and spewed fuel out and the exhaust was right there on the left side, below where the two pilots sat.

"Well, I was on the operations evaluations team when that helicopter was certified, and there were two things that I would not approve. One of them was the fact that the emergency exits were the two pilots' windows and the handles to release those emergency windows were in an indent and the indent was too small to get a gloved hand into. You would usually wear gloves but I didn't in this particular case because we were in such a hurry. I said if they ever have to get out in a hurry, they are never going to get their hands in there to get that handle to pull it out and jettison the windows. My boss overruled me. The second thing I would not approve was the shoulder harness arrangement. It was a Davis harness and it would never be approved today because now we require a single point release for your seat belt and shoulder harness. This one, the shoulder harnesses come over like suspender straps and hook in the fitting on the seat belt. So you had to release the seat belt and then get a hold of the shoulder straps and unhook them from this fitting.

"When we hit and that thing caught fire, neither one of us could jettison the window; we couldn't reach them. We were leaning on one side when the left gear collapsed and all our weight was on the shoulder harnesses and we could not get the shoulder harnesses unfastened. Struggle, struggle, struggle. In the meantime we are on fire and there is a lot of magnesium in the helicopter for saving weight. I don't know how Jim Lunn got out but I kicked my way through melting magnesium and aluminum. I never used an emergency exit; I kicked my way through the side of the helicopter with brute strength and got out. Of course I was in a state of shock and was dazed and now the helicopter and both of us are in a big gas spill that is on fire with flames probably four or five feet high. Jim Lunn had gotten out, how he got out I don't know, they never did figure out how he got out.

"He was sitting in the fire doing this [patting his arms]. I pulled him out of that fire and got clear of the fire spill and here comes a fire truck. We were no more than, oh a good drive and a five iron from the firehouse. Here comes this fire engine. Humongous tires."

Harry's memory flashed back to that night and in the expression on his face I could see that he was seeing the tires again, and he was horrified. When he began to speak again, tears rolled down his cheeks and his voice quivered. It was 1956 again.

"And this is my nightmare still. Up on the top is a fireman putting on a special white suit and those tires came right at me, I grabbed Jim and we rolled out of the way, we were both on fire. How the hell, it's a night dark as pitch, only the light of the fire, how the hell that tire missed us I don't know, but the tire missed us and they proceeded to put the fire out. One of the firemen saw us and took care of us.

"I received second- and third-degree burns as did Jim Lunn, him mostly third. We were taken to the North Shore Community Hospital, both of us, in two different ambulances.

"They initially gave us emergency treatment in the American Airlines clinic in the American Airlines hangar. But the skin was hanging off my hands; I could see bones. This was November and I was one of the founders of the Long Island Oratorical Society and I was accompanist for it. We were getting ready for our Christmas program and in about two weeks we were going to do a major piece and I kept saying, 'Who the hell is going to play for them?' That was all I seemed to be worried about.

"They gave me emergency treatment and they put me in an ambulance and I can remember the doctor saying, 'Keep him warm, he is in a state of shock, keep him warm.'

"So they piled me with blankets and they turned the heat up in that ambulance to the point where I couldn't breathe. It was so hot I kept yelling, 'Turn the heat off, I'm dying!' Well, they figured I was in a state of shock I didn't know what I was talking about, so they put on more heat! Well, I'm still screaming for them to turn the heat off and open the windows and let me get some air; I could hardly breathe because I had serious smoke damage in my lungs.

"The drive from LaGuardia Airport to North Shore Community Hospital in Manhasset is probably at least a half-hour drive. All this time I am dying of the heat. Finally, we pull up into a brightly lighted area and I'm saying to myself, 'Oh, my God, I might actually be able to get out of this damn furnace I'm in.' I thought we were at the hospital, but instead of that I heard the driver say, 'I'm going to fill her up while we are here.' We were in a damn gas station! The ambulance had taken a guy in a bad emergency to the hospital, and had to stop for fuel!

"We finally got to the hospital and I was put under the care of a wonderful doctor named Dr. John Mountain. He was a specialist in burns and he did the RAF WW II treatment of warm saline solution baths and an oxygen tank.

"A lot of the guys from the airlines at LaGuardia lived on the north shoreline, Manhasset and Great Neck and further up the island, and they would stop in on their way home from work to see me. One of them brought a case of booze; another one brought in some girly flicks. Dr. Mountain came in my room one evening, there must have been twenty people in my room and we were watching a girly flick, I was in an oxygen tent and the room was filled with cigarette smoke. Well, he raised holy hell, but there wasn't much he could do! But those guys would stop in and have a drink on their way home and see how I was doing.

"Well, poor Jim Lunn. The day we had that accident, which was November 30, 1956, his wife, they already had one child, was in the same hospital we were in giving birth to twins. I guess that's how life is perpetuated; life goes on. Jim lasted thirteen weeks and died. Every time I went down to see him he said, 'You're going to file a violation against me aren't you?'

"I said, 'No, Jim forget about it just get well!'

"Well, he died of his burns.

"When I got well enough to leave the hospital in December, John Mountain, the doctor, said, 'I want you to go to Florida, for at least three months, I want you in warm weather for the next three months.'

"I said, 'Well, hell I'm not a doctor, I work for a living, I'm a government clerk, I can't afford to go to Florida for three months!'"

Harry's voice broke again.

"He said to me, 'If you can't afford it, [silence] I'll pay for it.'"

It took Harry a minute to regain his composure.

"That wasn't necessary, the CAA gave me a set of orders that I was to proceed to Florida and I was to visit every military base on the way down there that had a helicopter operation to discuss helicopter operations and swap ideas and so forth. I did that with my wife Norine and two kids, until the weather warmed back up, up north.

"One of the weird things about John Mountain was he was a chain smoker. He always had two cigarettes, one in his mouth and one he was using to light the one in his mouth. He never stopped smoking. He was chain smoking and was talking to me when I got out of the oxygen tent, and he asked about my smoking habits. I told him I light a pipe up when in get up in the morning and knock it out when I go to bed at night and in between I smoke two packs of cigarettes. He said, 'You would be a damn fool to ever smoke again because of the damage to your lungs from the heat and smoke.'

"Well, that was good enough for me, I never put another one in my mouth. I lived in Freeport at the time and I had a neighbor who was a pipe smoker and he always admired my collection of pipes that I bought all over the world from my travels. Meerschaums from Germany, Dryers from England, and I got a big cardboard box and I put all my pipe racks, my tobacco humidors carried them over and said, 'Here, be my guest. Enjoy!'

"The *New York Daily News* had a front-page headline of this accident. Well, the article claimed that I had an opportunity to depart this helicopter, which was about to crash but I said to the pilot, 'I'm with you!' Where the hell they got that from I don't know! So this rabbi called me up and asked me if he could use that for the theme for his next sermon. I said, 'That's not what I actually said in fact we had no time to communicate with one another it happened so fast.'

"He said, 'Well, that's alright, I'm going to use it anyway if you don't mind.'"

"I've been in four major accidents, and the normal person might wonder why I'm still flying. But the normal person doesn't understand the addiction to flying the people who love flying have. When I retired in 1975, that was my last major accident, I thought that was enough flying for anybody but of course the damn fool I am I had to buy an airplane and keep flying, which I'm glad I did. It gives me a purpose in life and something to play with down at the airport and it keeps me out of the house and out of Joan's hair!"

6
CAA

While Harry was performing his reserve duties, he took a job with United Airlines flying DC-3s out of Denver to Chicago. While he was on a break he received a call from his mother back east in Connecticut.

"Son, you have a telegram," his mothers' voice spoke on the line.
"Oh, what's it about, read it to me," Harry responded.
"'If still interested, would you accept a position with the Civil Aeronautics Administration as an air carrier inspector, Grade GS12, $4,995 per annum. If interested, report to 385 Madison Avenue at 08:30 Monday morning.'"
It took Harry a second or two to fully comprehend who the telegram was from and what it was in reference to. Harry now explains this telegram came, although a bit later than he expected, just at the right time.

"That telegram, which was in 1947, was born from a trip I made to Washington, D.C., in 1944. Between flying the North Atlantic, we had shuttle duty. It went from Patuxent River, Maryland, to Washington then to Norfolk, Virginia.

"One afternoon, about a half a dozen guys got on my flight and I said, 'Hey, what are you guys going to Washington for?'

"'Well, we are going to apply for jobs as CAA inspectors.'

"I said, 'CAA inspector, what the hell is that?'

"They explained it to me and when I got to Washington, I conveniently had a slight mechanical problem that would delay my departure about thirty minutes. The CAA headquarters was about a five-minute walk up the hill, at Washington National Airport at the public works building. So we went in there and all filled out applications and were interviewed. When we were finished he told me, 'You will never be hired by us, you are too young, you have wonderful experience, but you are too young.'

"He told me they don't hire inspectors until they are at least thirty. So I forgot about it until this telegram three years later.

"Well, I was very interested because in those days, United and all the other airlines had hired so many military pilots that they had a glut of pilots. So they had a system called furloughs. I was furloughed more than I was flying. I would fly a week and have two weeks furloughed, then fly ten days and have three weeks furlough. My wife, Norine, and I had one daughter, Susan, who was about fourteen months old at this point, and we were living back with my family in New Haven, Connecticut.

"I went to my chief pilot, this was Friday evening by the way, and you could always get the jump seat, just tell them your mother was sick or something, but I could never lie to anybody about anything. I said, 'It's personal I can't tell you.'

"I couldn't tell him I wanted to go back for a job interview! So I couldn't get the jump seat without telling them what I wanted it for. Instead, I got in my 1942 Plymouth, blue four-door sedan and started driving the 2,200 miles back to New Haven without stopping. I did actually stop, I couldn't stay awake, but by Sunday night I was dead on my feet and I slept for about three hours, woke up and continued on my way.

"I got into New Haven about three o'clock Monday morning. Of course, everybody got up and we sat around the kitchen table, talking and drinking tea. Norine asked, 'Well, what does this entail?'

"I told her that if I am hired, I would make about twice as much money as I am making now and it will involve four or five weeks in Washington, D.C., indoctrination at headquarters, five or six weeks at Oklahoma City for flight training course and standardization course, then I will be assigned to a region.

"'Oh,' she says, 'We have been separated all this time, but if that is what you want to do then I will agree on one condition, that we buy a house trailer and you take Susan and me with you.'

"I said, 'Fair enough,' and bought a thirty-three-foot house trailer, dragged it down and parked it in Alexandria, Virginia. I went to the headquarter training there and then drug it out to Oklahoma City, parked it in a trailer park out there and then headed back to New York after that flight training program was over. Everybody was fairly happy, it was a nice trailer and that old 1942 Plymouth dragged that trailer all the way, never had a problem.

"Anyway, back to the interview. I freshened up a little bit and left at six o'clock to go to New York for my 8:30 A.M. interview; it was about a two-hour drive.

"I reported to the girl at the reception desk that I had an 8:30 interview. She said she would call me when they were ready, so I sat down and promptly fell asleep. Finally she came over and said, 'Are you alright?'

"I said, 'Yeah, I'm alright but I haven't slept since Thursday night, I'm just tired!'

"She said, 'Oh, you poor boy, come with me.'

"So she took me down the hall in to the nurses office and put me on the examination table and said, 'I'll call you when they are ready.'

"Well, I slept and they didn't call me until the middle of the afternoon. I had the interview and things weren't going too well. The chief of the flight standards division, which is the job I later had at the end of my career, interviewed me, as well as the chief of the air carrier branch. W. W. O'Connel was the division chief and the branch chief was Jerry Mulligan. He asked what I did for recreation and when I told him music was my hobby and that I played piano, I was in; I was hired."

CAA

Harry finished up quickly with United in Denver and made his way eastward back to New York. He, Norine and their daughter Susan eventually landed at the only trailer park at that time on Jericho Turnpike on Long Island.

He would have little time to get settled though, his new job awaited with the CAA at LaGuardia Airport. His first day on the job was, to say the least, interesting, but I should let Harry continue….

"I reported to the LaGuardia Air Carrier District Office on Memorial Day, 1947. Shortly after I reported in at 8:30, I got oriented, met everybody, was assigned a desk, went to lunch, got back from lunch and a United Airlines DC-4 with I think forty-something people on board crashed almost on the airport at LaGuardia. My first job was to investigate that accident.

"The airplane was a United Airlines flight that was taxiing out in a thunderstorm that was coming in off the northwest corner of LaGuardia. The captain asked the tower for an expedited departure to get out before the thunderstorm. Well, they expedited him and he sped out to the runway.

"On the Douglas DC-4, the controls are locked with a lever in the floor, just to the right of the captain's seat. When you pull this lever up to the vertical position you reach overhead and there is a spring loaded reel of red tape about three inches wide with a pin on the end of it. Well, you reach up, bring the pin down and put it in a hole in the lever so the lever stays locked. That red tape comes right down over what we call the throttle quadrant, where your four throttles, four propeller controls and your four mixture controls are located. So in order to get to those throttles you would have to pull that red tape out of the way to advance the throttles to full power. He never really got airborne obviously since the controls were locked, he went across Grand Central Parkway; this was on runway 18, which is no longer in use. He left the runway and got airborne enough to jump the Grand Central Parkway and roll his wheels across the top of a car of a TWA captain coming in to take his flight out. It crashed on the other side of the parkway into the parking lot of the Casey Jones School of Aeronautics. It burned and about half of the passengers got out and the other half were killed; the crew got out as well. That was my first day on the job and my first job was to investigate this horrible flaming DC-4 crash. That was Friday.

"United Airlines called the captain in to their office, he was a man of about fifty and they said we have computed your future earnings for this company, here is a check, get out of our face! He then went to work as a captain with Trans-Ocean Airlines, which operated out of Hartford, Connecticut, and he never crashed an airplane again.

"Often, when you make big mistakes like that you are never going to make that mistake again, you learn your lesson. It is just like people in aviation say there are two kinds of pilots, those who have landed with the gear up, and those who have yet to land with the gear up, and I don't believe that philosophy."

I agree. I noticed when I had the opportunity to fly with Harry, even though he had landed thousands of airplanes on all kinds of runways around the world, he still used his checklist. It was sort of a small clipboard affair that strapped to his leg and he called out the procedures as needed.

I was once on the scene of a gear-up landing, whereby the pilot was asked what happened. "The radios went out!" he said, "I didn't know what to do." We all stood there and wondered what the radios had to do with his gear and someone asked why he hadn't at least manually lowered the gear. "This plane doesn't have that feature," he said, to the astonishment of the gathering crowd. In the meantime, a crane had hooked the plane by the propeller and fuselage and began to lift it a few feet off the ground. One of the service technicians on hand climbed in the swaying plane and pumped the gear down and the crane gently returned the plane to the tarmac. I was hooking the tug to the front wheel, when I heard the pilot exclaim, "Well, I'll be damned!" Turned out this fellow was an instructor ferrying this plane, which was new to him, up from another local flight school for teaching the retractable gear lessons at the flight school at the airport. He was put on desk duty and I hope he never got the chance to pass his ignorance on to others. In any event, Harry's first weekend on the job was far from over.

"The next day, Saturday, Eastern Airlines took off from LaGuardia with a DC-4 on a flight to Washington, D.C.. It was a beautiful Saturday morning. Also coming up from Washington was a CAA airplane with CAA and CAB [Civil Aeronautics Board] people on it to help with the investigation. The CAB people, in addition to the economic regulations of the airlines, being before deregulation, were also charged by congress under the Civil Aeronautics Act of 1938 as amended, with determining the cause of the accident. The CAA people do a lot of the investigation in the areas of pilot proficiency, because we certified planes and shortcomings in aircraft design et cetera.

"They were coming up in a twin Beechcraft, which is six or eight passengers, and they were below the DC-4 and they were all looking up at it saying how pretty an airplane it was. While they were watching it, these were accident investigators, the airplane nosed over violently and went straight into the ground. It was in the vicinity of Conowingo Dam. To this day, the cause of that accident has never been established.

"The interesting part of that particular accident, was that the pilot of that Eastern flight was a Naval Air Transport Service pilot during WW II; I knew him. He was assigned to flight-test the new big four-engine flying boat; the Mars that Martin was building. They were shooting touch-and-go landings on the Chop Tank River off of the Chesapeake Bay and they were on their final approach, possibly less than 100 feet in the air, and the plane suddenly nosed down, hit the water at a forty-five-degree angle and porpoised before it came to rest; but nobody was hurt. So what a coincidence!

"That was late in the war, probably about 1945 and here it is now 1947 and another airplane diving but this one he did not survive, neither did anybody else. That was Saturday; my second day of work.

"The next day, a Capitol Airlines DC-4 coming into Washington, D.C., at night, tried to stay underneath a thunderstorm and ran into that mountain in Leesburg, Virginia. That was three days in a row; we lost three DC-4s, everyone was killed except for about half the people on the first flight. That became known as the 'black weekend,' I believed they called, it for a long time.

"Back to the other crash, where it nosed straight in, the control surfaces on the DC-4 were fabric. Many, many years later Allegheny Airlines was flying from Birmingham to Cleveland and they were over the Pittsburgh area, it was at night, and they were on cruise control. Everyone was relaxed when suddenly the airplane dove; pitched violently nose down. They were able to recover and land at Pittsburgh, to change shorts!

"Well, people thought of Eastern Airlines, May of 1947. Ah, ha, now we know what happened, they thought. What had happened was that the trailing edges of the control surfaces have strips of fabric glued onto them. On one side, the glue had let loose and that whole piece of fabric came off and acted like a damn tab, and threw the airplane violently down. So they got the remains of that DC-4 (from 1947) and all the fabric trim strips were intact, so that was not the cause of that crash after all."

Several other crash investigations stand out in Harry's mind. One, during the training of a new employee and another because it resulted in Bell helicopters rethinking the way they plugged in their starter cables.

"One of my early crash investigations was the crash of a United Airlines DC-6 with six pilots on board on a pilot training mission at Nagonset Field in Islip, New York. It killed all six pilots; it crashed right on the airport. Apparently, the trainer had pulled one engine back to simulate an engine failure on takeoff with the critical engine, which is number one, and the engine went into reverse. It's not supposed to but it did and the airplane just went straight down.

"A fellow by the name of George Van Epps had just been hired by the CAB as an accident investigator and he had no training and no idea on how to conduct an accident investigation, so he and I drove out together.

"We were the first people there besides the local tower operators and the medics. The first thing we had to do was take note of the instrument readings, sometimes they tell you an awful lot. Then we needed to establish the position of the throttles, the props and mixtures and the fuel selectors. In this case, in order to get instrument readings we had to scrape some brains off these instruments. They had already removed the bodies but there was blood and guts all over. So I trained George Van Epps on his first accident, of course he did many more after that. And so did I."

"One sad accident I investigated was the Port of New York Authority. They were headquartered in about a fifteen-story building in Manhattan. They called me up to investigate this helicopter accident; it was a Bell helicopter. They had a helicopter platform on top of the building and the pilot was in a hurry to get off, he was all by himself, and he did not unplug the big starter battery cable. In those days, the plug was plugged in to the side of the helicopter so if you left it in there and took off, the thing would not release. If you took off you would fly to the end of the cable and boom.

"Well, he went right down the side of the building; it was a terrible accident. As a result of that, Bell modified the receptacle for the starter cable to the bottom of the helicopter so if you took off with the starter cable plugged in it would pull out when you rose up. Those are the little things you learn from accident investigations.

"Accident investigation was only one of the functions of the air carrier inspector. We had to approve all the airports and sometimes we ran into difficult problems. Wilkes-Barre, Pennsylvania, was one I remember real well. The airport was sitting in the bottom of a big bowl and these mountains went up at a forty-five-degree angle all around that airport. In the daytime it wasn't bad but in the night it was horrible, it was nothing but black. So we finally wound up putting reference lights around those hills so the pilots had some reference points as they took off and landed at night. At that time we examined all the tower controllers and issued them their operating certificates, it later became the air traffic controllers' responsibility to do their own people."

Harry's days weren't always filled with investigating accidents. Some were rather routine, which I suppose is part of every job, even one that started so frantically for Harry. He explained just what he was tasked to do and even spilled a bit of philosophy on the subject of dealing with close calls.

"Most of our days were spent giving the airline pilots flight checks, six-month instrument competency checks that were required by the regulations for being a pilot. When a pilot gets updated to a new piece of equipment, we have to give what is called a type-rating check, which consisted of an oral examination and a flight check. We would pick up a pilot at LaGuardia and perhaps give him a line check to Tulsa, Oklahoma. We would spend the night in Tulsa and come back the next day and catch another crew. We were normally given one leg to fly during the trip from the left-hand seat and I remember flying a Convair 240 from LaGuardia to Albany, then to Syracuse, Rochester, Buffalo to Detroit to Battle Creek, Michigan to Chicago.

"I was giving the captain a line check and he gave me, it was the middle of winter; snowing everywhere, the worst weather to fly from Detroit to Grand Rapids, Michigan. We landed in the middle of a snow squaw and the wind was very high. I have forgotten the exact numbers of the runway, one of them was a west heading and the other was a northwest heading, let's say it was runway 27 and runway 32. The wind was severely out of the northwest but within the limitations of the airplane. When we broke contact, I had so much crab on it, that even though I was landing on runway 27 I was lined up with runway 32 because of the crab. I started to correct my drift to get lined up with the runway and he took it and said, 'No, this way!'

"And I said, 'No, this way!'

"Well, we split the difference and landed in-between the runways. There was lots of snow piled up and it was a very bumpy landing and noisy. We got back on the runway and Mike Glerum, the captain says, 'I'll never do that again!'"

During all those years Harry was giving flight checks, he told me that he never flunked an airline pilot. Now, before you question his integrity on this matter, you must understand that Harry would have never done anything to endanger the life of any passenger or, for that matter, an industry that Harry loved. Harry could tell, in some of the cases that the pilots were almost afraid of him, of the chance that they might be permanently grounded on the whim of the CAA inspector.

There was one pilot that Harry remembers during this time that was a special situation ....

"I was giving a line check to a DC-6 captain from Tulsa, to Memphis, to Nashville, to Washington, D.C., to LaGuardia. It was a night flight. Sometimes we spent the night in Tulsa and sometimes we just got on another eastbound flight and came back. The captain's name was Joe Hammer. I noticed when I got aboard, after we introduced ourselves, the first officer had four stripes, which meant he was a captain. So we got into approach Memphis and the first officer said, 'Joe, listen, I haven't landed this runway in a long time; let me make this landing.'

"So the copilot made the landing. Actually a reserve captain is what they called him. The same thing happened when we got to Nashville, he said to Joe, 'Hey, there is a pretty good crosswind, I haven't had a crosswind landing in a while, let me make this landing.'

"The next stop was Washington, D.C., that was the leg they gave me to fly.

"Joe Hammer was up sitting in the jump seat. It was a beautiful night and we were letting down and I was passing through 1,900 feet MSL when Joe shook me on the shoulder and said, '900 feet is too low, get some altitude.'

"The reserve captain said, 'Joe, that is 1,900 feet, not 900.'

"'Oh, excuse, me.' Joe said.

"So we landed and when we got to LaGuardia, the reserve captain made the landing; there was some excuse. When I got to the office the next morning and I was looking at my notes, and I was making out my report, I realized that I had line checked this captain and never seen him land the airplane. So I called Walter Braznell and said, 'I would like to talk to you about my pilots.'

"So we set up a time and I went over that afternoon and he asked what the pilot's name was.

"'Joe Hammer,' I said.

"And he went over and closed the door.

"I said, 'Walter, I just line-checked him, four stops Tulsa to LaGuardia, I never saw him land the airplane, the reserve captain made every landing except for the one I made.'

"He said, 'Yeah, it's a sad story, Joe Hammer has cancer and it affects his eyesight, but he is the best-liked pilot on the system. He is a gunsmith, on his flights he picks up guns and puts new stocks on them, reblues them, everything free of charge.' He said, 'We'll let him go as long as he can, but we will always have a safe flight, we will always have a reserve captain as copilot. You don't have to worry about safety, I guarantee you it will be a safe flight.'"

So Joe Hammer continued to fly, it was probably the last, best thing he could have done for himself. He died about a year after Harry's check ride with him without incident. Friendly skies Joe....

"Also at the time I was an air carrier inspector at LaGuardia, in fact it was the first year I was an inspector, all of TWA's overseas operations came under what they called the intercontinental division. There was the domestic division and the intercontinental division and they were just getting Constellations. In 1947, they were doing their flight training at Wilmington, Delaware. We were doing up to six type-rating flight checks a day. One day I got so exhausted from this schedule, even though I was a young fellow of twenty-seven, I called my boss at LaGuardia and said, 'I've had it, I'm too exhausted, I can't handle dawn patrol.'

"He said, 'Well, you come on home and we'll send Puck Dawson,' who was another Navy buddy of mine.

"So I went home and Puck went down, and the very first flight the next morning, the aircraft was a Constellation with six on board, four TWA pilots, the flight engineer and the CAA inspector Puck. They landed short and hit a little berm and flipped the airplane on its back. It burned so badly that they didn't even know who was in what seat. So I came very, very close to buying the farm there.

"A lot of guys can't handle that and get out of the business. I was always able to close the door on the history part of it and go on with the new program. You know, after some serious accidents you would think I would learn my lesson, but here I am still flying. Today they bring in counselors to council, like they do in school when some kids die, they bring in counselors to make them feel comfortable with what happened. We didn't have counselors we just dealt with it, whatever happened, happened just don't make the same damn mistake again!"

Harry became chief of the flight standards division in 1968 and was assigned to the New York office. Several years prior to his moving back, an "organizational genius" (tongue firmly planted in cheek) decided to decentralize the organization and add another layer of supervisors he called the "area concept." This meant that the United States would be divided into sections, each having several headquarters from which to operate within each region.

A fellow named Jim Ship called Harry one day while he was painting the highest peak on his house. Harry didn't want to take the call because he knew if he got down from the ladder, he would never get back up there to finish the job.

Jim insisted and the peak never got painted. After talking with Jim for a while Harry was basically given the option to go to New York or Cleveland. Harry wanted no part of New York. He had put in his ten years there and wanted something else, so he ended up in Cleveland doing flight checks and other duties such as type rating airplanes and the like.

Eventually the "area concept" died and at that time Harry was contacted by the regional director for what was the northeastern region. He was being promoted to chief of flight standards, but in New York. Harry balked. He wanted nothing to do with New York any more.

He was told he would have two weeks to come up with a good reason why he wouldn't be promoted and brought to New York. Two weeks later Harry was in New York with a new job.

Harry's time in New York was, to say the least, difficult. He didn't really want to be there and there was another problem that few, if any, people were aware of. His wife, Norine, had developed into an alcoholic and took Valium to combat depression.

It was a hard question to ask but I needed to know what happened, if only to gain a better understanding of Harry.

"Norine never drank, at least in the early days. It was later on she developed the drinking problem and I know what caused it, or at least what I believe caused it.

"Down the beach from us there were two couples from the squadron. One of them was Albert H. 'Pete' Odell and his wife Louise. He had one leg. He graduated from the Naval Academy and he worked on our flight control department. He left his leg on a New York parkway returning home from the USS *Prairie State*. It had been converted into a training center and he taught there. Louise lived in Mt. Vernon, New York, and he was taking her home after some kind of Naval function and in the wee hours of the morning he was coming back and there was a stalled car; the fellow had run out of gas. Well, Pete stopped to help him and said, 'Yeah, I'll take you to a gas station, but let's get your car off the road before somebody hits it.'

"While the two of them were behind the car pushing it, a car came down the road and hit them. It cut his leg off right above the knee about halfway up the thigh. The guy that drove the car never once came to see him in the hospital. He used to tell about his honeymoon night when his wife reached down there and touched his leg and passed out. He loved to tell that story, I don't know if it's true but he loved to tell it.

"They lived in a house down the beach from us with another couple and they got in a big fight and they came knocking at the door and asked if they could stay in one of the bedrooms. So they stayed with us for quite a while and we became good friends.

"During the Korean War when I was recalled to active duty, I was based up at Argentia Naval Air Station in Newfoundland. And I can't remember exactly where I was, either Newfoundland or in Thule, Greenland, when somehow Norine got through to me by telephone, but I couldn't understand her. Not because of the connection but from the way she was talking. It didn't occur to me she was drunk because she never drank. She called to tell me that Louise had died in childbirth and I guess it was just too much for her to handle. So I came home to see if I could help her out.

"Well, she had a problem with alcohol ever since. She could not get out of that bottle. She did join Alcoholics Anonymous, which is the only successful way to beat that disease. She became quite active in it, she wrote a lot of their pamphlets; she was a very bright woman. She was sober for quite a while until we transferred from New York to Washington in 1957 and she did pretty well down there but she had a few slips. Then we got transferred from Washington to Cleveland and that is when she had her big problem.

"You know, when a man is transferred in his business from city to city he can handle it, it is part of his career development. You don't realize what a tremendous trauma it is for the wife and family at home. When we moved back to New York that was the end of it, she died in New York. Died from alcohol and drug abuse. The doctors put her on Valium as treatment and they overdosed her on Valium. She died in 1972, when she was forty-nine."

It was sad to see Harry's heart break all over again when he told me about Norine. I had no idea Norine died under such horrible circumstances.

After the devastating loss of his wife, Harry did what he could to move on, although his life would never be the same without her.

It was only three years after Norine died that Harry put in for retirement. He was fifty-five years of age and had more than thirty years of service and that meant he was eligible for retirement. I am sure Harry was looking forward to the easy life.

The Washington office approached Harry to stay on for another six months until the first of July, 1975, so they could find a replacement. Even though he could see the waves and feel the sea breeze of retirement just around the corner, Harry reluctantly agreed. He shouldn't have.

"When I was working up in New York I got a new boss, and at the time, I basically had my own airplane based in Long Island Republic Airport, N6, a DC-3. He wanted to take a three-day trip and visit some of the offices in the northeast region, which was all right with me; I'll use any excuse to fly.

"We had eleven of his staff plus him so it was a dozen total passengers. I took a fellow by the name of Carl Peterson who was my check airman and instructor pilot for that particular airplane as my copilot. Normally when I fly with a qualified copilot, we will swap legs; I'll fly left seat the first leg, then he'll fly the left seat the second leg. But we had trouble with the seats sliding up and down the tracks, so when I went to move the seat back, he said, 'Oh, you stay and fly from the left seat.' So I stayed and flew from the left seat.

"We had a trip that went up to Stewart Air Force Base and the weather was putrid. We shot our RVR [runway visible range] approaches there, visited the people and then went up to Albany, couldn't get into Albany the weather was on the deck. Then we flew over to Rochester; couldn't get into Rochester. Then we went up to Niagara Falls and got into Niagara Falls and spent the night there; the weather still putrid. The next day we went from Niagara Falls to Erie, Pennsylvania, shot an RVR approach there, then to Morgantown, West Virginia, the weather was a little better there, but not much. We met the officers, then flew up to Allegheny Airport in Pittsburgh, met the people there, then went to Greater Pittsburgh and spent the night.

"The next day the weather improved and in the meantime, this fellow that was my new boss was nagging me to let him fly the DC-3. I said, 'Are you qualified to fly the DC-3?'

"'Oh, yeah, I fly it all the time out of hanger six at Washington National Airport.' That is the FAA hanger. So he convinced me that he was qualified. The third day we took off and went to Erie, Pennsylvania, and attended a luncheon there, the Kiwanis, or Rotary or one of those civic clubs. We went up there to give 'We Point with Pride' plaques to a flight service station employee that had talked down a student pilot who had gotten caught up on top of the overcast and couldn't get down.

"After lunch we took off and I said to my boss, 'OK, this is your leg.'

"We were going to Harrisburg to meet with the state aviation officials. The weather was now beautiful, and the wind was right down the runway. He got in the left-hand seat and I told Carl I was going to be in right-hand seat.

"Naw, you have been flying for two days solid, relax, I'll stay over here.'

"So I was back on the flight deck and on the DC-3 there are probably twelve feet of mostly radio racks and little radio operator's table there then the door that goes into the cabin. I was standing by the door going through the log books making sure that they were complete and up to date. On take off the left engine quit, and I heard Carl yell, 'I've got it!' and I went forward to see what the hell was going on.

"We were about 100 feet in the air, now going straight down. I dove on the floor back towards the cabin door, and when we hit, those radio racks and everything caved in on me and busted open the front of the airplane; the two pilots were hanging out in the open air in their seat belts. I was trapped, it took them an hour and a half to cut me out, and I was lucky it didn't burn.

"Everyone was taken to the hospital, but the only ones that had to stay were my boss in the left seat, Carl in the right-hand seat and myself. The others were treated and released. I wound up a couple weeks in the hospital there, with a broken left wrist, a broken left elbow, tore all the ligaments and tendons in my right leg. I was in a cast from hip to ankle for several months, but I got over it.

"An interesting thing when we hit, I lost my shoes, I lost my wristwatch, my eyeglasses, everything. I told the FAA people I lost my Bulova watch among other things. Several months later they put out bids for the wreckage and the highest bid was $254.00. The guy who bid on that came with a crane and a big flat body truck and when he was turning the fuselage over the watch dropped out.

Harry pulled up his red and black flannel shirt to reveal the watch. It had a new crystal and a new band since then, but it was still ticking after that licking....

"I got a call from the flight service station manager up there and he said, 'What kind of watch was it you lost?'

"I said, 'It was a Bulova.'

"He said, 'We got it, it dropped out of the plane when they loaded it on the truck.'"

"There was a fellow that used to write for the Washington papers; he was a rumormonger. He wrote a column about the, 'So-called safety experts' of the FAA who went to Dubois, Pennsylvania, to give an award to one of the flight service station personnel. They were honored by the rotary club or the lions, one of the two at which time there was quite a bit of drinking going on.'

"Now is that inflammatory or what? None of us had a drink. He continued, 'These so-called experts got in their DC-3, took off and rolled down the runway like a drunken sailor and these so-called safety experts crashed the airplane.'

"As a result of that, the congress people got a hold of that article and they were all over the FAA, they wanted them to do something drastic about the crew, especially the pilot in command. I was the pilot in command, but I wasn't flying the plane, but I was the pilot in command because my name was on the flight clearances as pilot in command.

"The first night I was in the hospital I got a call from my assistant Brian Vincent, who was the assistant division chief. Apparently he had more information than I knew he had because he said, 'The FAA is only going to ask you one question tonight; who was flying the airplane?'

"I said, 'I already told you earlier in the evening that I was flying the airplane.'

"He says, 'Harry, you better tell them the truth because it's going to come out sooner or later, don't lie about it, tell them the truth.'

"So when they came in they asked me the one question and I told them who it was.'

"They said, 'Thank you.' And they left.

"Somebody had to shoulder the blame, as pilot in command I had to shoulder the blame because of the FAA regulations the pilot in command is responsible for the safety of the flight. I met with them in Washington and they said, 'We are going to suspend your air transport license for ninety days, do you have a problem with that?'

"I said, 'No.'

"I had already put in for retirement when I turned fifty-five in January of that year and they talked me into doing another six months until they got a replacement. I told them that I didn't intend on flying as captain on an airline so I didn't need the airline transport rating and I said, 'Well, you have to do something and that is reasonable.'

"So they suspended my airline transport license for ninety days and that seemed to satisfy everybody."

There is one interesting side note to Harry's time as an air carrier inspector. To say he did a lot of flying would be the same as saying Einstein could do math. They are both true, but you don't necessarily understand the depth of either.

During this time, Harry had a particular string going and he told me that he might be the only person left in the world who can say this. It's impossible to prove, but indeed he may be the only man left who has flown the DC line of aircraft from the DC-3 to the DC-10, including the very rare DC-5. I knew the DC-5 was a rare bird and asked Harry to tell how it all came about.

"I happened to fly a DC-5 when I was in the Navy. They only built twelve of them and when the war came along the Navy bought most of them. The Navy called them the R3D. It was a tricycle-gear high wing, if you would describe it today you would call it a corporate aircraft. It was not built for airline service; it was built for the heads of the airlines, of Boeing aircraft, et cetera. It was equipped with leather seats and leather sofas and a bar and toilet and so forth. It was a very plush interior.

I flew that in 1943. That was one of the airplanes before I was designated a Naval aviator in this period of ninety days in which I was assigned to operations in Norfolk flying everything.

"It turned out by the time I was ready to retire, I had flown and was type rated in the DC-3, DC-4, had flown the DC-5 but wasn't type rated, DC-6, DC-7, DC-8 and the DC-9. I was about ready to retire and got a call from a chief pilot of American Airlines, Dan Weatherby, and he said, 'Hey Harry, how would you like to add the DC-10 to that string of yours?'

"I said, 'Yeah, I would love to, what's up?'

"He said, 'Well, we got a training squadron that got its first DC-10 and were going to go up; go with us. We won't be able to give you enough training to get a type rating in it but I'll let you fly it so you can say you have flown the DC-10.'

"So we went out and did some touch-and-goes at the end of Long Island. I may be the only man in the world that has that string from the DC-3 to the DC-10, since the DC-5 is on there and not many people got to fly that one. That's not much of an accomplishment after seventy-nine years of life!

"One of our local pilots lives down in Murrells Inlet, South Carolina has an A-36 Bonanza he keeps down in Georgetown, South Carolina. He asked me about that string and he said, 'You know I've got a good friend over in Columbia that owns a DC-2.'

"I said. 'DC-2, I didn't know a there were any around.'

"He said, 'Yeah, he has one, he has a little museum and has six different airplanes and one is a DC-2 and he keeps a full-time mechanic on the payroll and keeps it airworthy. He flies it during his annual, so maybe we can talk him into letting you fly it so you can add the DC-2 to the bottom of your list.'

"I said, 'Well, E.J., that would be wonderful, I would love to do that, but I didn't realize there were any damn DC-2s still flying.'

"So maybe that will happen, maybe it won't."

Whether or not Harry adds the DC-2 to his list of DCs I don't know. I do know that he has put an awful lot of time in the DC fam-

ily of airplanes and considers them some of the finest flying aircraft in the world.

Harry had finished flying for a job. His countless hours in the air and at the desk were enough. He decided that in the sun would be where he retired and chose a little village called North Myrtle Beach, South Carolina.

7
GOLDEN YEARS

Retirement was good for Harry. He played golf, and was very active in the church, playing both piano and organ and also singing. He eventually joined a group of singers named the Grand Strand Singers and in this group were two people who were to play very important roles in Harry's retirement. First, the choirmaster, Don Hamacher was a pilot and owned a 1964 Piper Twin Comanche. Well, that was all right with Harry. After knowing Don for some time, he asked Harry to go in "halves" with him on the plane and now Harry had his own plane. And a good one at that.

The other person that Harry became close friends with was my grandmother, Fayaline Mims. She had retired to North Myrtle Beach about the same time and lived just a short walk from Harry. It was through my grandmother, whom we called "Mimey" that Harry was introduced to my aunt Joan, Mimey's middle daughter.

Without going into all the gory details, that's how I ended up moving to Oak Island, North Carolina, just about forty-five minutes north of North Myrtle Beach in 1998 to begin this book.

One evening as we sipped hot tea in the living room, I asked if he knew where any of his old logbooks were. Rocking out of his chair, he instructed me to follow him downstairs to the sun room. Opening *and closing drawers of a dresser he remarked,* "I know they are in here somewhere, jeez I haven't thought about those in a long time..." *whereupon the last drawer he opened revealed three small stacks of green, brown and black logbooks.* "Oh, here they are," *he said and pulled one off the top and flipped through it remarking that it was from somewhere in the 40s.*

He pulled eleven books out in all and handed them to me. When I got home that evening, I spent the better part of four hours flipping through the books and generally being amazed that nearly every flight he made was recorded in those books. They include his very first flights right through his solos and check rides. Also included were his crash in Chad in 1942 along with various entries that helped me nail down events and try to put things in some sort of chronological order. There were, however, two entries that made me scratch my head. One because it happened at the airport that was literally two miles from my house on Oak Island and because they both had "Drug Aircraft" for a comment. I asked Harry about these and he filled me in on the details.

"I got familiar with the local DEA man up there in Wilmington, North Carolina, and he worked closely with the Wilmington police department. I got a call from Lieutenant Turner of the Wilmington police who asked me if I could taxi a DC-4 off the runway at Brunswick County Airport in Oak Island and I said I could. At that time, Brunswick was a sod strip, 3,000 feet long, and has since been paved and lengthened. So I went up there the next day and sat in the cockpit to familiarize myself with it. I checked later in my logbooks and the last time I flew the DC-4 was 1948. So that's thirty-two years since the last time I sat in the cockpit of a DC-4.

"Well, I probably had 3,500 hours in DC-4s, Navy R5Ds. After sitting there for about ten minutes it was as if I had just flown the airplane yesterday and landed it and taxied it in. Everything just fell right into place. To start the engines, for example, each engine, on the overhead switch panel, had three switches. The one in the middle was to rev up the starter, the one on the right was a boost pump to give it fuel and the one on the left was to engage the starter. I was able to reach up without looking and start all four engines successfully. I taxied the airplane off the runway and parked it over at the terminal area.

"It is interesting how that airplane got to be in the middle of that runway. There was a retired ATF agent that had retired in Long Beach, not far from the airport. He got bored with retirement and joined the local police department. He was heading home after work one morning, about 1:00 A.M., and heard a large airplane fly overhead. Well, with his experience he thought there has got to be something funny going on at Brunswick County Airport. So he called his police headquarters and told them he was on the way to the airport and told them what his suspicions were. He was armed with a .38 Special in a shoulder holster and went on out to the airport, and sure enough there was a drug airplane sitting right in the middle of that sod strip. It had flown up from Colombia nonstop and there is a high powered NDB [non-directional beacon] called Carolina Beach that operates at 216 kilohertz and you can pick that up down there. All you have to do to fly a load of drugs out of Colombia is tune your radio to 216 kilohertz and home in on it and there is the airport.

"When he got to the airport, there was a lot of activity. They even had floodlights to unload the airplane. They had semitrailers, they had pickup trucks; they had all kind of vehicles. There must have been about seventeen people unloading that plane. He walked up and he said to one of the men, 'Is this good quality stuff?' And the reply was, 'This is some of the best quality stuff we have ever seen.'

"So he backed off and in a loud voice, after whipping out his .38 Special said, 'It's the police, everybody on the ground!'

"Well, they had all kinds of weapons, including automatic weapons. Instead of blowing him away, they all laid down on the ground. Now what the odds are against that I don't know! But I will say this; he had guts with a capital 'G.'

"About this time the police had shown up and they arrested everybody, they also picked up a gas truck that was on Route 211 that was on its way to refuel it. The next day Lieutenant Turner called me and asked me if I would taxi the airplane off. Well, after I taxied the airplane off, I said, 'You know Lieutenant, if you want this airplane over at Wilmington at the DEA compound, I could fly it over there for you.'

"He said, 'Can you do that?'

"I said, 'Yeah, but I can't do it now, it's too hot.'

"I suspected it was in pretty good shape because although it was a DC-4, it had DC-6 gear and brakes on it for heavy loads and good stopping. I said, 'I'll do this at dawn patrol tomorrow morning.'

"Well, I drove up there at sunup and one of the fixed base operators at Wilmington was there and the biggest thing he had flown was his own Twin Comanche. He asked if he could be the copilot and I told him I would be happy to have him. The DEA put an agent on board, I guess so I wouldn't steal the airplane!

"So I started the engines and taxied down to the end of the runway and ran the engines up. You run those engines up to thirty inches of manifold pressure and do a magneto check. I continued to go through the checklist, most of it from memory. I lined it up on the runway and was going to make a practice run first to see if the engines would perform and see if I could get enough airspeed to go. I said, 'If I get seventy-five knots before I reach the midpoint, I am going to throttle back and taxi back and we'll line up again and I will take off.'

"Well, I had seventy-five knots, because the airplane was light there were only three people on it, at about a quarter of the runway. I said to Ed Samuel, 'We're out of here!'

"We took off and climbed out. I didn't retract the gear because it was modified and I didn't know that they would operate properly, although I assumed they would since they had come up from South America. Well, Brunswick County Airport to Wilmington can't be more than about a five-minute flight so I gave Ed instructions on how to fly a big airplane. When I figured we had done enough dilly-dallying around I headed on to Wilmington.

"I had no pilot handbook of any kind so I had to rely on memory as to what the speeds were. It came to me just as if I had flown the airplane yesterday. It was 120 knots downwind, 110 knots on base leg, and 100 knots across the fence. I followed those speeds and made a beautiful approach to runway 24 at

Wilmington and that may have been one of the best landings I have ever made in my life in that airplane, not having flown it for thirty-two years.

"I looked over at Ed and he looked at me and he had a big grin on his face and I said to him. 'Any questions Ed?'"

After Harry told me this story, I figured I should ring up the local paper, the Pilot, *from Southport, North Carolina, and see if I could find an article. Ten minutes after walking in the office of the* Pilot, *I had in front of me an article written by Elizabeth Hammond about the event. In the photograph section of this book you will find a reprint of this article and although the photo might be a little fuzzy, I bet if you look hard enough you will find Harry giving the DC-4 a pre-flight inspection.*

That, however, wasn't the only brush with drug aircraft Harry had. About six months later, in January of 1981, the local DEA agent approached him again, this time to ferry a plane from Asheville County Airport. Harry continues.

"Asheville County Airport was a new airport they had built on top of a mountain near Boone, North Carolina. They just cut down the top of the mountain and built a 3,600-foot runway there [which has since been lengthened]. This involved a DC-6 that had come up from Colombia with drugs and had landed on this new strip. The fellow that flew that plane had a more flight time flying thunderstorm penetration, for the U.S. Weather Bureau, than most pilots get in their life. He had 16,000 hours of thunderstorm penetration research. He had retired from the Weather Bureau and he got involved in running drugs, not so much for the money, although the money was outstanding, but really because he was bored with retirement and he wanted something to do. So he would go over to Tacos Corner at Miami International Airport and there would be an envelope on a bulletin board with all the information; where the airplane would be, a key to a locker where the money would be after delivering the load and so on. Well, he flew this trip into Asheville and they unloaded and everybody disappeared except the pilot; he had a drinking problem. He was at a local bar that evening and the bartender said to him, 'Hey buddy did you hear about the airplane that came in here with a load of drugs?'

"And like a braggart he said, 'Not only did I know about it, I was the pilot!'

"The bartender says, 'Come on, don't BS me.'

"He said, 'Yeah I flew it, I came in earlier today.'

"About ten minutes later here comes the sheriff. He sat down next to the pilot and said, 'Hey fellow, I understand you're the pilot of that load of drugs that came in this afternoon.'

"Yeah, I was the pilot of that airplane, why?'

"'Why? Come with me.'

"That airplane of course was confiscated and the pilot eventually got a suspended sentence for that flight and I'm sure he went on to fly many more drug loads. In any case, that airplane sat on top of that mountain for I think twelve or fourteen months so the airplane was in pretty bad shape. The thing that will deteriorate a piece of equipment more than anything else is lack of use. The DC-6 had fabric control surfaces so they were all in bad shape and some had rotted away. I got a call from the drug enforcement people, and asked if I could fly that airplane into Wilmington, I said, 'Yeah, if you can get the airplane airworthy I will fly it in for you.'

"So they put a crew up there in charge of fixing it. When they called me and told me the airplane was now in airworthy condition according to the foreman of the crew, I flew my airplane up to Wilmington, parked it and got a ride up to the top of that mountain. I put on my coveralls and went over that airplane with a fine-toothed comb to satisfy myself. When I finished my inspection, I said to the foreman of the maintenance crew, 'Go get your bag, you're going to be my flight engineer on this trip.'

"His eyes popped out and he said, 'Me!'

"I said, 'Yeah, you told me that airplane was airworthy, so prove it!'

"So we went and the airplane worked fine. We put the DC-6 into the Wilmington DEA compound and I got in my airplane, my trusty little Twin Comanche, and flew down to Myrtle Beach. When I walked into my condominium, my phone was ringing. I picked it up and the voice at the other end of the line said. 'Are you the pilot that flew the DC-6 into Wilmington?'

"I said, 'Yeah, how did you know that?'

"He said, 'We had a crew on top of that mountain, we were going to steal the airplane again, we had everything in position to steal it tonight.'

"'So we followed you to Wilmington, saw you get in your Twin Comanche and followed you down to Grand Strand Airport. We asked the fellow in the terminal who that fellow was in the Twin Comanche, he gave me your number and I'm calling you with this offer: We will pay you upon delivery of the drugs, $150,000 cash for one round trip.'"

Ahem...

"One round trip from here to Colombia and back is about twelve hours, so that would be a very lucrative hourly rate."

Try $12,500 an hour...

"I said, 'Not interested.'

"As much as I was tempted to say, for the first time in my life, I am going to knowingly do something that's illegal, I thought about it then I said to this fellow, 'I've spent my whole life promoting aviation safety and the FAA regulations and am not about to do a crazy thing like this, thanks a lot, but no thanks. And he hung up."

I never doubted for a minute that Harry would turn a cold shoulder to the offer. He had spent too many years on the right side of the law and morality to have it all end like that. Anyway, Harry had his own forms of "busy work" to keep him out of trouble. He had his Twin Comanche, his condo by the beach and a membership at Bay Tree Golf Plantation. What more could a retired fellow ask for?

His Twin Comanche would take him nearly around the world at his whim. From trips to the Sun and Fun fly-in in Florida to visiting his very good friend Eddy Frankiewicz in San Diego, Harry flew as often as he could. He loved the air; he was born to fly.

GOLDEN YEARS

He continued to sing in local choirs and even during the time he sat down to do these interviews, was regularly singing. A philatelist, he holds an impressive collection of rare and interesting stamps. And although in my youth I considered stamps boring, I changed my mind the evening Harry shared his enthusiasm with me.

Yes, retirement was going as Harry planned, in his words, "Waking up in the morning not knowing what I am going to do that day and going to bed not having gotten it done!"

That is until one cool November day when the postman delivered a letter from his nephew wondering if he had ever thought about writing a book.

8
EPILOGUE

At the outset of this project I knew I would be in a race, but little did I know how fast a race I would have to run in order to fulfill my dream of getting a finished copy of this manuscript to Harry before his last foray into the wild blue yonder.

Almost two years after I conducted my final interview with Harry and nearly a year after I thought I would have this project finished, Harry suffered health problems, some of which stemmed from his 1956 helicopter crash at LaGuardia Field, New York, which limited his ability to get around as well as he did for his eighty-year-old frame. Things weren't looking so good and I wondered if I would be able to deliver an even somewhat finished product to Harry before his Hobbs meter quit counting.

I was especially worried when in July of 2002, Harry did what we all thought he would never do; he sold his trusty Twin Comanche. It was such an important day for Harry and Joan and all of his airport bum friends, that the local paper covered the event, making front page news replete with a picture. Shortly thereafter, I received in the mail a large envelope containing a copy of the North Myrtle Beach Times *with a hand-written note from my aunt Joan paper-clipped to the front.*

EPILOGUE

> "After 63 years of flying and 27 years flying the Twin Comanche - in Harry's words, the end of an era - Wanted to share this bittersweet day with you - Hope all is well, Love to you both, Joan and Harry"

As I read the note and looked at the picture on the front page showing Joan and Harry waving goodbye to N7495Y as it taxied to the runway, I, like everyone else that knew Harry, feared it wouldn't be long until Harry made his own final departure.

I worked diligently on the book and on January 27, 2003, was able to FedEx Harry a copy of the manuscript which had by then, taken its final form and was as complete as I felt I could get it given the situation. Some months prior, Harry had suffered more health setbacks that left him weak and in constant need of attention and was confined to a hospital bed placed in his house in North Myrtle Beach.

I was relieved to get a call the following afternoon from Joan saying that she had gotten the package and had been reading some of it to Harry. She said Harry was very happy to be able to see the manuscript and then she asked if I would like to talk with him.

His voice was weak and his breathing labored, but it was still Harry, the same jovial, cherubic-cheeked fellow that I had grown to love so much, especially over the past few years. He said he appreciated all the hard work on the book and as he paused to catch his breath, and with tears in my eyes, I told him that it was all my pleasure and that I would see him soon. He said he loved me and I told him the same, and that was the last time I heard Harry's voice.

Harry Bernard died on February 9, 2003, surrounded by love and with the knowledge that he lived his life to the fullest.

I was asked to speak at Harry's Memorial Mass at Our Lady Star of the Sea Catholic Church in North Myrtle Beach, South Carolina, and as a final tribute to a man who had become one of my heros, I wrote the following eulogy:

> When Harry was a child, around three or so, he was playing on the deck of the apartment in which his family

EPILOGUE

lived in Scotland. He had climbed up on the rail and was balancing himself, walking across, sort of like a tight rope. His mother, seeing this, ran over and grabbed him before he fell. While she held him, his grandmother, whom they called "Granny" said, "That boy will go high in life."

It must have been some sort of intuition, because that is exactly what Harry did with his life; go very high.

Some people are put on this earth to race cars or play professional sports. Some to become doctors or nurses, teachers or engineers. Harry was born to fly.

From his first solo in 1941, to his last logbook entry not too many months ago, his sixty-three years in the cockpit netted some 35,000 hours in more than 130 different types of airplanes and helicopters. To put that in perspective, if Harry spent his time in airplanes as a normal eight-hour work day, that would amount to fifteen years solid in the air. That's not counting his work on the ground. Indeed, Harry was born to fly.

His career spanned the globe and at the age of twenty-two he ferried equipment across the belly of Africa with Pan Am. Along the way he had a crash landing on the banks of the Ubangi-Shari River in French Equatorial Africa with a load of .50-caliber ammunition to be used against Rommel in the North African campaign. They got caught in a thunderstorm and lost one engine and were forced to coax the plummeting airplane into some sort of landing. He was subsequently rescued, flown back to base and continued flying his missions.

He was a member of the first Naval Air Transport Service squadron, VR1. During this time he flew the North Atlantic routinely and carried all kinds of interesting people, even Charles Lindbergh once.

On one of those North Atlantic flights Harry located and organized the rescue of the crew of a downed B-17. He told of the helpless feeling he had while he circled those crew members until help arrived. His bril-

EPILOGUE

liant work and determination saved the lives of several crewmen and earned him the Navy's Commendation Medal. That was nearly sixty years ago and when Harry told me the story, he cried. Even though he did all he possibly could, given the situation, Harry felt as though it wasn't enough because all the crew wasn't saved.

He worked for the FAA as an air carrier inspector, administering flight checks and insuring the safe designs of aircraft before they went into production. During this time Harry received his Air Transport License, which stated that all aircraft type ratings were authorized. That license, which isn't even issued anymore, basically meant if it had wings he could fly it. And Harry did.

But all that flying came with its own price. A crash during a check ride Harry was giving in which the pilot-in-training made an incredibly hard landing, resulted in Harry having to kick his way out of the melting body of a Sikorsky helicopter, pull the pilot-in-training to safety, and dash out of the way of the tires of a fire truck coming to his rescue, all while engulfed in the most horrible flames. Those images haunted Harry for the rest of his life as well as leaving his lungs and legs badly burned. A crash on takeoff in a DC-3 in Pennsylvania left him with a broken wrist, arm and torn tendons in his leg. But as Harry told me, "I got over it." Nothing could keep Harry out of the air, as I say, Harry was born to fly. It was an addiction, he once told me.

He also loved golf, which is one of the reasons he settled here in North Myrtle Beach. I remember playing with him once at the Bay Tree Golf Plantation in 102-degree heat. My dad, brother and I spent the day chasing balls and generally looked like hackers while Harry would wait patiently in the cart, his ball on the short grass. With almost every shot Harry would turn and through smiling teeth say, "Not long, but straight." Needless to say, Harry whooped us that day.

EPILOGUE

And music. From the time he was a child, Harry was involved in some sort of musical endeavor from piano to singing in the choir. At one time he was soloist at Trinity Church on the Green in New Haven, Connecticut. While there he met one of the greatest organists of all time, and it made quite an impression on young Harry. Marcel Dupre was the organist of the Notre Dame cathedral in France and a master of his craft. During a stateside organ recital tour, Marcel played at Trinity Church. Harry sat next to him on the bench and turned the pages as music filled the hall.

Throughout his life Harry played for many churches, including the Lakeside Baptist church right here in North Myrtle Beach. It was after a performance during a fellowship meeting while Harry was gathering his music from the organ and about to leave the bench when the pastor asked him to stay and play something while the congregation bowed their heads in prayer. In Harry's words:

"Well, if you have ever seen your best friend and can't remember his name, that's what happened to me. My mind went completely blank. I don't play by ear so I have to have music in front of me, that or I have to have memorized it, one of the two. So I just didn't know what to do in that situation, but I looked up and everybody had their head bowed waiting for me to do something and I said to myself, 'Bernard, you have to do something!' Well, I couldn't think of what to play, not even 'Stand up, Stand up for Jesus,' or 'Onward Christian Soldiers.' So in desperation I sat down and played 'Smoke Gets In Your Eyes.' But I played it very reverently. It was the only song that popped into my mind; it was a song I had memorized years before. So I played it and put a nice little 'amen' at the end of it thinking some of the people would overlook the song I was playing if it had a nice 'amen' at

EPILOGUE

the end of it. Well, when I finished, the Pastor, Jim Mezick said, 'That's beautiful, a little unusual, but beautiful and maybe that's a reminder not to let the devil put smoke in our eyes.'"

But it was airplanes that captured his soul. The roar of the props, the smell of the exhaust and the smooth slip sliding on a carpet of clouds is what Harry loved. His airport buddies will attest to that. I flew with Harry not too many years ago while I was spending some time down here interviewing him for his biography. Each Wednesday I would travel down and spend the afternoon, most times long into the evening talking and peeling the years away to expose those wonderful stories. During the first of those three-month long Wednesday meetings he mentioned that if we had the chance we might go for a fly. That was all right with me. I had flown with Harry nearly ten years earlier and would welcome the chance to do it again. There was only one thing… I don't do so well in small planes, sometimes the bumps just seem to get to me. Well, Harry never knew it but from the first meeting on, every Wednesday before I left the house, I took a dose of Dramamine just in case that would be the day we would fly. I wanted to be prepared at all costs and getting sick in Harry's airplane was something I wanted to avoid.

So it was on the second to the last meeting with Harry that as we were driving back to the house from dropping a friend off, Harry turned to me and said, 'How would you like to go for a fly?' I'm not sure who was more toothy, me or Harry. We turned into the airport and before I knew it we were airborne. We flew up the coast and around Smith Island, not talking much but just enjoying the flight. Even though at the time, Harry had just turned seventy-nine, I swear when I looked over at him he couldn't have been much older than thirty.

EPILOGUE

As we neared the airport for our landing, things got a little rough due to ground roll turbulence. The little Twin Comanche bounced and slid through the air, the whole time autopilot guiding us in. As things got a little worse and the Dramamine started to wear off, Harry said, 'I can do better than this,' and flicked off the autopilot and smoothed us out. His hands and feet moved with a quickness and assuredness of a man who has done this a thousand times before. 'Don't worry, you're flying with the world's greatest pilot.' He joked, but I knew he might very well be.

We landed smoothly and taxied the airplane to the hangar. On the ride back to his house we didn't say much but we were both happy and we both still had that toothy grin. I'll always remember that flight, just Harry and me. It was the highlight of my time with Harry, to be with him as he did something he so enjoyed; to see him in his element; to see him young again.

Indeed the end of an era is upon us. Harry was in no uncertain terms one of a kind. And he touched the lives of everyone who came in contact with him; your presence bears witness to that.

Harry, the skies are now yours. You have been granted your final clearance for takeoff. The winds are in your favor and the sky is clear. We love you dearly and will miss you longingly. So long my friend.

But, if you happen to look up one cloudless day and see one of those white vapor trails streak through the sky but no airplane in sight, wave. It's Harry, just stopping by to say hello and to let you know he's doing just fine.